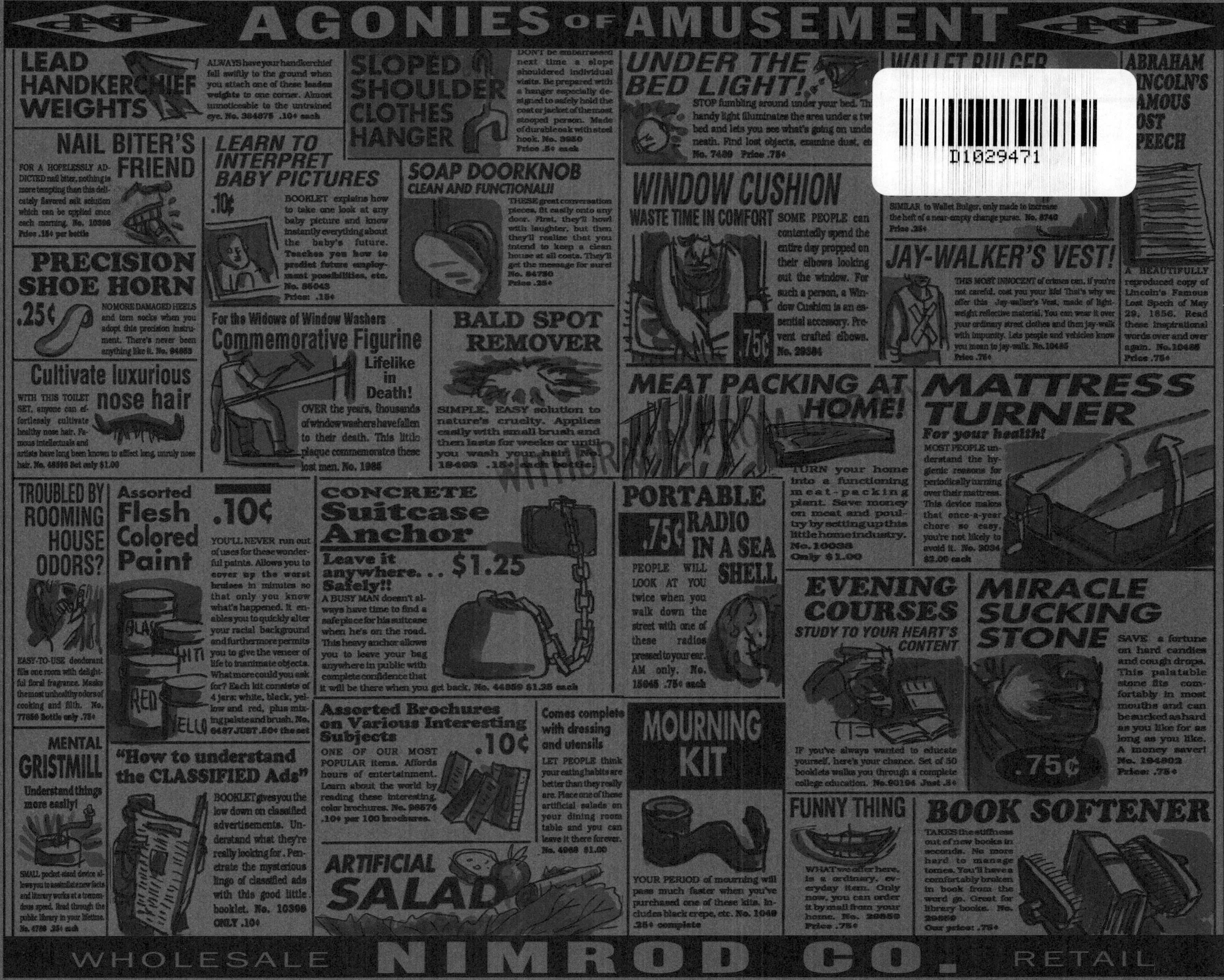
AGONIES OF AMUSEMENT
LEAD HANDKERCHIEF WEIGHTS
ALWAYS have your handkerchief fall swiftly to the ground when you attach one of these leaden weights to one corner. Almost unnoticeable to the untrained eye. No. 384875 .10¢ each
SLOPED SHOULDER CLOTHES HANGER
DON'T be embarrassed next time a slope shouldered individual visits. Be prepared with a hanger especially designed to safely hold the coat or jacket of the most stooped person. Made of durable oak with steel hook. No. 3850 Price .5¢ each
UNDER THE BED LIGHT!
STOP fumbling around under your bed. This handy light illuminates the area under a twin bed and lets you see what's going on underneath. Find lost objects, examine dust, etc. No. 7489 Price .75¢
ABRAHAM LINCOLN'S FAMOUS LOST SPEECH
A BEAUTIFULLY reproduced copy of Lincoln's Famous Lost Spech of May 29, 1856. Read these inspirational words over and over again. No. 10468 Price .75¢
NAIL BITER'S FRIEND
FOR A HOPELESSLY ADDICTED nail biter, nothing is more tempting than this delicately flavored salt solution which can be applied once each morning. No. 10398 Price .15¢ per bottle
LEARN TO INTERPRET BABY PICTURES
.10¢
BOOKLET explains how to take one look at any baby picture and know instantly everything about the baby's future. Teaches you how to predict future employment possibilities, etc. No. 85043 Price: .15¢
SOAP DOORKNOB
CLEAN AND FUNCTIONAL!!
THESE great conversation pieces, fit easily onto any door. First, they'll howl with laughter, but then they'll realize that you intend to keep a clean house at all costs. They'll get the message for sure! No. 84780 Price .25¢
WINDOW CUSHION
WASTE TIME IN COMFORT
SOME PEOPLE can contentedly spend the entire day propped on their elbows looking out the window. For such a person, a Window Cushion is an essential accessory. Prevent crafted elbows. No. 29384
.75¢
SIMILAR to Wallet Bulger, only made to increase the heft of a near-empty change purse. No. 8740 Price .25¢
JAY-WALKER'S VEST!
THIS MOST INNOCENT of crimes can, if you're not careful, cost you your life! That's why we offer this Jay-walker's Vest, made of lightweight reflective material. You can wear it over your ordinary street clothes and then jay-walk with impunity. Lets people and vehicles know you mean to jay-walk. No.10485 Price .75¢
PRECISION SHOE HORN
.25¢
NO MORE DAMAGED HEELS and torn socks when you adopt this precision instrument. There's never been anything like it. No. 84683
Cultivate luxurious nose hair
WITH THIS TOILET SET, anyone can effortlessly cultivate healthy nose hair. Famous intellectuals and artists have long been known to affect long, unruly nose hair. No. 48598 Set only $1.00
For the Widows of Window Washers
Commemorative Figurine
Lifelike in Death!
OVER the years, thousands of window washers have fallen to their death. This little plaque commemorates these lost men. No. 1985
BALD SPOT REMOVER
SIMPLE, EASY solution to nature's cruelty. Applies easily with small brush and then lasts for weeks or until you wash your hair. No. 18493 .15¢ each bottle.
MEAT PACKING AT HOME!
TURN your home into a functioning meat-packing plant. Save money on meat and poultry by setting up this little home industry. No. 10038 Only $1.00
MATTRESS TURNER
For your health!
MOST PEOPLE understand the hygienic reasons for periodically turning over their mattress. This device makes that once-a-year chore so easy, you're not likely to avoid it. No. 3034 $2.00 each
TROUBLED BY ROOMING HOUSE ODORS?
EASY-TO-USE deodorant fills one room with delightful floral fragrance. Masks the most unhealthy odors of cooking and filth. No. 77850 Bottle only .75¢
Assorted Flesh Colored Paint
.10¢
YOU'LL NEVER run out of uses for these wonderful paints. Allows you to cover up the worst bruises in minutes so that only you know what's happened. It enables you to quickly alter your racial background and furthermore permits you to give the veneer of life to inanimate objects. What more could you ask for? Each kit consists of 4 jars: white, black, yellow and red, plus mixing palate and brush. No. 6487 JUST .50¢ the set
CONCRETE Suitcase Anchor
Leave it anywhere. . . Safely!!
$1.25
A BUSY MAN doesn't always have time to find a safe place for his suitcase when he's on the road. This heavy anchor allows you to leave your bag anywhere in public with complete confidence that it will be there when you get back. No. 44959 $1.25 each
PORTABLE RADIO IN A SEA SHELL
.75¢
PEOPLE WILL LOOK AT YOU twice when you walk down the street with one of these radios pressed to your ear. AM only. No. 15645 .75¢ each
EVENING COURSES
STUDY TO YOUR HEART'S CONTENT
IF you've always wanted to educate yourself, here's your chance. Set of 50 booklets walks you through a complete college education. No.90194 Just .5¢
MIRACLE SUCKING STONE
SAVE a fortune on hard candies and cough drops. This palatable stone fits comfortably in most mouths and can be sucked as hard as you like for as long as you like. A money saver! No. 194802 Price: .75¢
.75¢
MENTAL GRISTMILL
Understand things more easily!
SMALL pocket-sized device allows you to assimilate new facts and literary works at a tremendous speed. Read through the public library in your lifetime. No. 4788 .25¢ each
"How to understand the CLASSIFIED Ads"
BOOKLET gives you the low down on classified advertisements. Understand what they're really looking for. Penetrate the mysterious lingo of classified ads with this good little booklet. No. 10398 ONLY .10¢
Assorted Brochures on Various Interesting Subjects
.10¢
ONE OF OUR MOST POPULAR items. Affords hours of entertainment. Learn about the world by reading these interesting color brochures. No. 98574 .10¢ per 100 brochures.
Comes complete with dressing and utensils
LET PEOPLE think your eating habits are better than they really are. Place one of these artificial salads on your dining room table and you can leave it there forever. No. 4968 $1.00
ARTIFICIAL SALAD
MOURNING KIT
YOUR PERIOD of mourning will pass much faster when you've purchased one of these kits. Includes black crepe, etc. No. 1049 .25¢ complete
FUNNY THING
WHAT we offer here, is a ordinary, everyday item. Only now, you can order it by mail from your home. No. 28850 Price .75¢
BOOK SOFTENER
TAKES the stiffness out of new books in seconds. No more hard to manage tomes. You'll have a comfortably broken in book from the word go. Great for library books. No. 29889 Our price: .75¢
WHOLESALE NIMROD CO. RETAIL

CHEAP NOVELTIES

CHEAP NOVELTIES

THE PLEASURES OF URBAN DECAY

with Julius Knipl, Real Estate Photographer

Ben Katchor

Drawn & Quarterly

WO2-34£5

JULIUS KNIPL

REAL ESTATE
PHOTOGRAPHER

3, VESEY ST

I STILL HAVE A COUPLE HOURS GOOD LIGHT

MR. KNIPL MUST QUELL HIS MEMORY OF WHAT PREVIOUSLY STOOD ON THIS SITE.

HERE, NUMBER 156. IT WAS THE GOULASH BUILDING.

IN A FEW MINUTES, THE SHADOWS WILL BE JUST RIGHT

AS HE IS ONE OF THE FEW MEN ONTO THIS RACKET...

SUN

EARTH

THE CREEPING SHADOW

HIS ANSWERING MACHINE IS ALWAYS FULL.

...A TEN-STORY BUILDING ON JUBAL AVE. ...I NEED SOME PHOTOGRAPHS...

HE RETURNS A PHONE CALL,

PLEASE, I DON'T WANT TO MEET YOU, JUST GIVE ME YOUR ADDRESS AND I'LL SEND YOU THE PICTURES

THINKS OF WHAT HE'LL DO WITH THE MONEY FROM THIS JOB,

A COLD BORSCHT

AND THEN BEMOANS THE CLOSING OF HIS FAVORITE DAIRY CAFETERIA.

AN IDLE ONLOOKER TERRIFIES MR. KNIPL.

SOUVENIR!? TAKE A PHOTO HOME FOR THE FAMILY! ONLY FIVE DOLLARS!

NO THANKS

5

IF FOUND RETURN TO:
JULIUS KNIPL
REAL ESTATE PHOTOGRAPHER
3. VESEY ST. WO2-3521
AND RECEIVE REWARD

A FLOPHOUSE?

FIDELITY HOTEL
A LINE HOUSE

IT MUST BE THE WRONG ADDRESS.

YES, THIS IS IT. THE OWNER WANTS PHOTOS OF THE PLACE.

IT'S THE LAST OF A CHAIN OPERATION.

HOPE HOTEL A LINE HOUSE

FORTUNA HOTEL
A LINE HOUSE

IT USED TO BE, STARTING UP IN THE THIRTIES ON SECOND AVENUE, YOU'D HAVE ROOMING HOUSES

ROOMS

THEN AROUND UNION SQUARE, HOTELS FOR TRANSIENTS

HOTEL

AND DOWN HERE ALL KINDS OF CHEAP FLOPS.

THERE WAS A PLACE FOR EVERYONE TO SLEEP.

NOW THAT THE WHOLE CITY'S A SKID ROW, NO ONE WANTS TO RUN A CHEAP HOTEL

I KNOW HIM.

FIDELITY HOTEL

HE'S THE NIGHT MAN AT THE AMBROSE COFFEE SHOP.

WHAT'LL YA HAVE?

JULIUS KNIPL
REAL ESTATE PHOTOGRAPHER
E. VESEY ST.

HOW CAN I GET A GOOD PICTURE!

WHAT'S THE BIG ATTRACTION?

MR. KNIPL RECALLS HAVING SEEN A CERTAIN TRUCK

LIVE FISH

AND UNDERSTANDS THAT SOMEWHERE UPSTATE THERE ARE FARMS

WHERE FISH ARE ARTIFICIALLY BRED.

IT'S ALL ACCORDING TO A PLAN.

FOR A MOMENT, HE CONSIDERS THE SENSELESS COURSE OF HIS OWN LIFE.

FOUR YEARS OF ALGEBRA

THE DANCE SCHOOL

A PONY-CART CONCESSION

THEN, I HAPPENED TO SEE THAT AD IN POPULAR MECHANICS.

EXCUSE ME, EXCUSE ME, I NEED A CLEAR FACADE!

Julius Knipl
REAL ESTATE PHOTOGRAPHER
3, VESEY ST.

EE YOWww

A SCREAM IN THE NIGHT REMINDS MR. KNIPL THAT SLAUGHTERHOUSES ONCE OPERATED ON THE WEST SIDE.

YAOWww

MOOoo

MATAS
WHOLESALE

VEAL

HE WONDERS WHAT BECAME OF HIS FRIEND GRINBERG, THE SHOYCHET.*

PHEW. YOU SMELL SOMETHING?

NO.

*KOSHER SLAUGHTERER

HE GAVE ME A RIDE ONE MORNING.

I REMEMBER HE LIKED TO SHOW OFF HIS SPECIAL KNIVES.

WITH THE AIR CONDITIONER ON, YOU COULD STILL HEAR THE ANIMALS.

ROOoo

EVEN THEN, HE DIDN'T HAVE WORK EVERY DAY.

AH! THEY'RE RUINING MY NEGATIVES!

SOMEBODY GIVES A SCREAM AND RIGHT AWAY THEY CALL THE POLICE

JULIUS KNIPL
REAL ESTATE PHOTOGRAPHER
3. VESEY ST.

WATER
SAMPLING
STATION
Nº 18

MR. KNIPL OFTEN NOTICED THESE WATER SAMPLING STATIONS AROUND THE CITY, BUT UNTIL NOW HADN'T SEEN ONE IN USE.

WHAT A JOB!

MANDIBLE RESERVOIR

CANDY CIGARS
SODA FOUNTAIN

A BAG OF SALTED PEANUTS, PLEASE

TE-A

SEVERAL BLOCKS LATER, ANOTHER SAMPLE.

MR. KNIPL BEGINS TO FEEL A PRESSURE ON HIS BLADDER.

INFERO-LATERAL A

WHAT A JOB

AH!

JULIUS KNIPL
REAL ESTATE PHOTOGRAPHER
MR. KNIPL SEES MEN BEING USED TO CARRY INCREASINGLY HEAVY LOADS.
IT'S INHUMAN!
A BREAKDOWN DISRUPTS HIS WORK.
THAT WAS ALREADY CRACKED.
I'M FINISHED. I CAN FEEL IT IN HERE. MY ABDOMINAL TRUSS SNAPPED.
IT'S A DISGRACE. YOUR BOSS SHOULD BE USING A TRUCK FOR SUCH WORK.
WHAT BOSS?! I CONTRACT SHORT DISTANCE MOVING JOBS MYSELF.
MY CUSTOMERS LOVE IT. IT'S PICTURESQUE.
HANDTRUCKS AND VANS ARE SO IMPERSONAL. DON'T YOU SEE THE APPEAL OF HAVING A STOOPED FIGURE CARRY YOUR FURNITURE THROUGH THE STREET?
MY SILENT SUFFERING ENNOBLES THEIR POSSESSIONS... I'M A HUMAN BEAST OF BURDEN, SCURRYING BETWEEN CARS AND BUSES, STARING DEATH IN THE FACE EVERY MOMENT... I CAN'T FIGURE HOW MANY POUNDS I HAVE TO HAUL TO BREAK EVEN... WITHOUT A LOAD, I STILL WALK BENT, WITH MY EYES TO THE GROUND AS THOUGH SEARCHING FOR MY GRAVE ... CAN THEY HEAR MY BONES BREAKING...

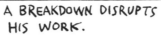

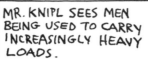

JULIUS KNIPL
REAL ESTATE PHOTOGRAPHER WKL 174
3 VESEY ST.

MUKIE RESTAURANT

SOMEWHERE, MR. KNIPL PICKED UP THE HABIT OF READING A NEWSPAPER STARTING FROM THE BACK.

HE EXAMINES THE NAMES OF HORSES AT SARATOGA...

STUDIES NEW DEVELOPMENTS IN TOUPEE SCIENCE...

NATURAL   ARTIFICIAL

SEES WHICH SHIPS ARE IN PORT...

READS AN OBSCURE DAILY COMIC STRIP...

by Hersh

MUST I BORROW THE MONEY IN FRONT OF THESE PEOPLE?

LOSES HIMSELF IN A ONE BY TWO INCH ADVERTISEMENT...

WHY SUFFER?

YES!

35

AND THEN FINISHES HIS COFFEE.

11

MR. KNIPL WAS SURPRISED TO LEARN OF THE TRADE CARRIED ON IN NEWSPAPER WEIGHTS.

HE FIGURED THESE WERE ODD SCRAPS OF IRON.

BUT NO! HEAVY-DUTY TRUCKS CRUISE THE CITY

AND CANDY-STORE AND NEWSSTAND MEN KNOW

THEY CAN GET DIFFERENT SIZES AND SHAPES.

I NEED A SEVEN POUND OSWEGO.

IT'S A BUSINESS THAT IS SLOWLY LOSING GROUND

DO YOU STILL CARRY THOSE TRIBUNE PANCAKES?

TO THE CHEAP ALUMINUM WEIGHTS SUPPLIED BY CIGARETTE COMPANIES.

YEARS AGO, YOU'D NEVER HAVE A PHOTO RUINED

BY A STRAY SHEET OF NEWSPRINT.

CLIC

A HEAT WAVE

I NEED AN ICE-COLD SODA.

MR. KNIPL WALKS FOR BLOCKS, PAST DOZENS OF STORES

AND COFFEE SHOPS SELLING REFRIGERATED DRINKS.

HE RECALLS AN OLD OBJECT,

THE SMELL OF BOTTLES FLOATING IN DARK ICE WATER
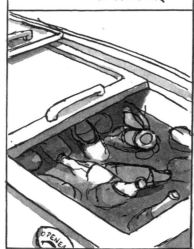

AND SEARCHING FOR A DEFUNCT BRAND OF SODA.

FINALLY, WAY UPTOWN.

13

TWEET TWEET

JULIUS KNIPL
REAL ESTATE
PHOTOGRAPHER
3, VESEY ST. WO2-1123

THE NEWSSTAND!

JUST LIKE THAT. THEY TOOK IT AWAY

IN THE MIDDLE OF THE NIGHT.

MR. KNIPL REMEMBERS THAT ONE DAY, MANY YEARS AGO.

IT WAS HOT

HESH'S CHOCOLATE & CHOCOLATE SYRUP

AND HE NEEDED A LOT OF WATER.

HE DISCOVERED AN IN-EXPLICABLE STAIN ON HIS SUIT,

SKULNIK FANCY MEN'S CLOTHING
TAKE A GOOD LOOK AT YOURSELF.

AT A CERTAIN TIME,

CASHEW BROS

HE BOUGHT DINNER

HOT SWEET POTATO 10¢

AND THEN PLAYED A GAME OF CHESS.

FINALLY, HE STOPPED TO HEAR A LECTURE PRE-DICTING THE END OF ALL STREET AMENITIES.

JULIUS KNIPL
REAL ESTATE
PHOTOGRAPHER
3 VESEY ST.
WO 2-1175

LANDMARK COFFEE

MR. KNIPL KNOWS OF A PLACE WHERE BLACK COFFEE FLOWS FROM THE WALL.

ONE REGULAR

IT'S THEIR SPECIALTY.

WHOOoo

OPEN 24 HOURS

THEY ALSO SERVE SANDWICHES

SARDINE SANDWICH & COFFEE $1.00

THE BEST COFFEE 35¢

WHAT A GIMMICK!

WHERE'S IT BREWED?

IN THE BACK?

IN THE CELLAR?

WHEN NO CUSTOMERS ARE AROUND, THEY RUN THE COFFEE FULL BLAST DOWN THE DRAIN.

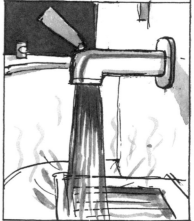

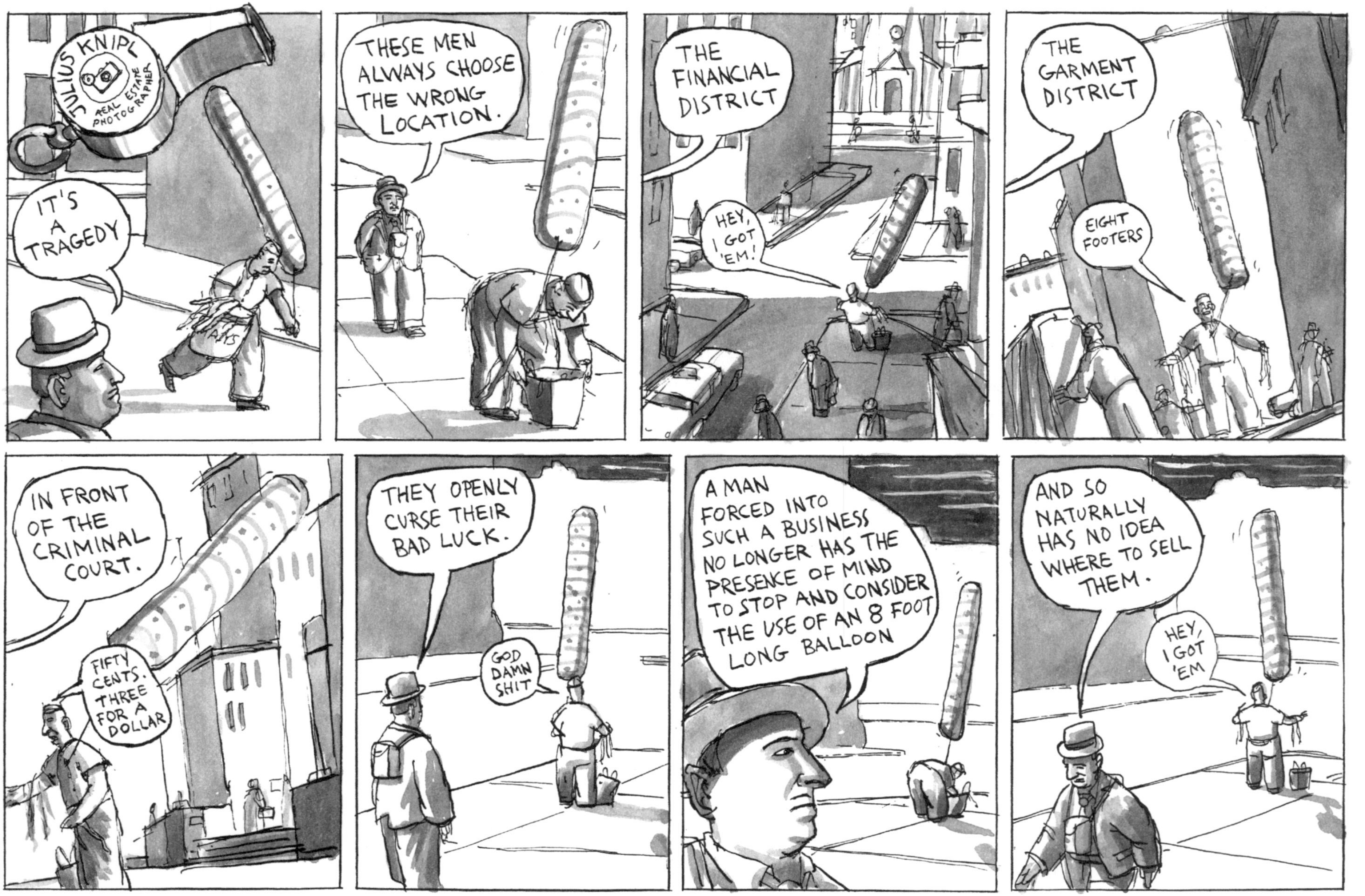
JULIUS KNIPL
REAL ESTATE PHOTOGRAPHER
IT'S A TRAGEDY
THESE MEN ALWAYS CHOOSE THE WRONG LOCATION.
THE FINANCIAL DISTRICT
HEY, I GOT 'EM!
THE GARMENT DISTRICT
EIGHT FOOTERS
IN FRONT OF THE CRIMINAL COURT.
FIFTY CENTS. THREE FOR A DOLLAR
THEY OPENLY CURSE THEIR BAD LUCK.
GOD DAMN SHIT
A MAN FORCED INTO SUCH A BUSINESS NO LONGER HAS THE PRESENCE OF MIND TO STOP AND CONSIDER THE USE OF AN 8 FOOT LONG BALLOON
AND SO NATURALLY HAS NO IDEA WHERE TO SELL THEM.
HEY, I GOT 'EM

ABE LUCKSHUN

AT THIS TIME OF YEAR, TELEPHONE BOOKS ALL OVER THE CITY...

BEGIN TO BUCKLE AND COLLAPSE UNDER THEIR OWN WEIGHT.

THE DISTINCTION BETWEEN THE WHITE AND YELLOW PAGES BECOMES UNCLEAR.

THE ADVERTISEMENTS SUDDENLY LOOK OUT OF DATE.

ONE MAN FINDS THAT THE PAGE HE NEEDS HAS BEEN RIPPED OUT.

OTHER PEOPLE ARE TEMPTED TO PERFORM A STRONG MAN STUNT.

MR. KNIPL HAS UN-CONSCIOUSLY SPARED ONE PAGE

FROM THE ANNUAL HARVESTING OF LAST YEAR'S PHONE BOOKS.

SEE THE SIGHTS!

1 HO BUS TOU

MR. KNIPL WAS SURPRISED TO SEE IT STILL IN BUSINESS

RUN BY THE SAME OLD COMPANY

THE DRIVER, AFTER 20 YEARS ON THIS ROUTE, MUST FORCE HIMSELF NOT TO SPEED

THE HOME BASE OF THE MAN IN . . .

OUT OF SYNCH WITH THE TOUR GUIDE.

THE GRAY FLANNEL SUIT.

ON ONE CORNER, THE BUS HAS WORN A GROOVE INTO THE ASPHALT.

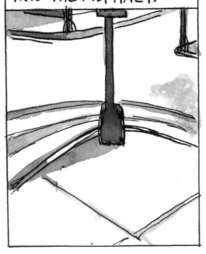

THE STARING EYES OF COUNTLESS TOURISTS HAVE EFFACED THE FRONT OF A FAMOUS STATUE.

TO MR. KNIPL, THE BUS ITSELF,

WAS THE ONLY POINT OF INTEREST IN SIGHT.

IT IS NOT, AS MANY PEOPLE THINK, PRIMARILY A PSYCHIATRIC HOSPITAL.

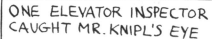

ONE ELEVATOR INSPECTOR CAUGHT MR. KNIPL'S EYE

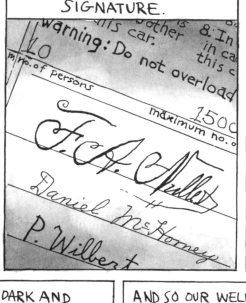

WITH HIS DISTINCTIVE SIGNATURE.

HE WAS HERE FIVE YEARS AGO ON APRIL 27

TO EXAMINE NOT ONLY THE ELEVATOR'S MECHANICAL OPERATION

BUT MORE IMPORTANTLY TO PEER INTO THE DISMAL VOID THAT LIES AT THE HEART OF MOST BUILDINGS.

THESE DARK AND FRIENDLESS SHAFTS ARE A NECESSARY ADJUNCT TO THE ECONOMY

AND SO OUR WELFARE DEPENDS UPON THEIR MAINTENANCE.

MR. KNIPL UNDERSTANDS WHY THESE MEN, OF ALL THE CITY INSPECTORS, DESERVE TO HAVE THEIR NAMES PUBLICLY DISPLAYED IN A SUITABLE, TRANSPARENT-FACED FRAME.

MR. KNIPL TRIED A NEW SALVE FOR HIS SORE EYES.

HE SOON BEGAN SEEING TANK TRUCKS CARRYING IT IN BULK.

HE'D SMELL A WAREHOUSE, ON THE OUTSKIRTS OF THE CITY, DEVOTED TO IT,

HEAR MEN FIGHTING OVER IT IN PUBLIC,

FEEL THE VIBRATIONS OF A MACHINE THAT PACKAGED IT

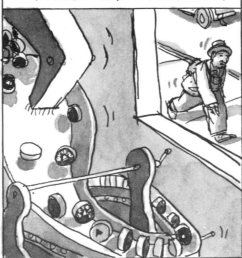

AND TASTE THE EXHAUST FROM A STATION WAGON FULL OF IT.

WHEN HE STOPPED USING THE SALVE, THESE APPARENT SIDE EFFECTS DISAPPEARED.

JULIUS KNIPL *REAL ESTATE PHOTOGRAPHER*

ANY CROWD IN THE THEATER DISTRICT IS BOUND TO CONTAIN AT LEAST TEN ELECTRIC SIGN WATCHERS.

PEOPLE HIRED TO KEEP AN EYE OUT FOR BLOWN LIGHTS

TO PROTECT AGAINST AN EMBARRASSMENT

NORTH WEST CORNER OF 47th

IT'S A NECESSITY, EVEN THOUGH THESE SIGNS ARE SEEN BY THOUSANDS OF PEOPLE EVERY DAY.

WHO WOULD REPORT A DARK LETTER OUT OF THE GOODNESS OF THEIR HEART?

SEVERAL BLOCKS AWAY, ON A LESS TRAFFICKED STREET

MR. KNIPL KNOWS OF A BLOW OUT, RESULTING IN A MEANINGLESS WORD,

STILL ON DISPLAY AFTER THREE MONTHS.

TO MR. KNIPL, IT'S NOT FROZEN CUSTARD,

BUT A HAUNTING MELODY, THAT THESE TRUCKS OFFER.

THE OPERATORS ARE OBLIGED TO HAND OUT SOME CONCOCTION

BUT IT'S THE CHIME-LIKE RECORDING,

PROJECTED THROUGH SMALL, EXTERNAL SPEAKERS, THAT CONCERNS THEM.

IF THEY DON'T ATTRACT A CERTAIN NUMBER OF LISTENERS, THEY MOVE ON TO ANOTHER STREET

AS THEY DID ONE SUMMER EVENING, TEN YEARS AGO.

JULIUS KNIPL
REAL ESTATE PHOTOGRAPHER

Poissy CORSET SALON

THAT'S THE GUY.

MAURICE DE POISSY, A SUCCESSFUL BUSINESS-MAN.

HE'S ALWAYS HANGING AROUND ON THE EAST RIVER BRIDGE

IS HE WAITING FOR ME TO GO AWAY?

SHOULD I NOTIFY HIS FAMILY BEFORE HE DOES SOMETHING DRASTIC?

LOOK, THE EFFECT IS IDENTICAL...

TO THAT OF A DRESS WORN OVER A WELL-MADE CORSET.

De Poissy CORSET SALON

YOU HAVE TO STOP AND LOOK.

IN THE SAME WAY A DOCTOR ASSOCIATES CERTAIN PHYSICAL SIGNS WITH THE END OF A HUMAN LIFE

MR. KNIPL KNOWS WHAT TO EXPECT AT THE LAST STOP ON ANY SUBWAY LINE.

A TROPHY MANUFACTURER

A MOVIE THEATER CONVERTED INTO A BUSINESS SCHOOL

THE OFFICES OF A WEDDING ORCHESTRA

A DIETETIC CANDY STORE

A BUS DRIVER'S UNIFORM AND SUPPLY STORE

HOWEVER, THESE LAST MANIFESTATIONS OF PRIVATE ENTERPRISE CAN LINGER ON FOR A QUARTER OF A CENTURY

AN ILLEGAL FRANCHISE OF A DEFUNCT FAST-FOOD CHAIN

OR LONGER.

A PLASTIC SLIPCOVER SHOWROOM

WHENEVER MR. KNIPL CONSIDERED BUYING NEW CLOTHES OR HAVING HIS HAIR RESTYLED

HE WOULD INEVITABLY RUN ACROSS A BEAUTY SCHOOL CARRYING CASE.

THESE CASES WERE FREE GIVEAWAYS

COMPLETE WITH STYROFOAM HEAD

USED TO ATTRACT NEW STUDENTS.

WHEN THINGS DIDN'T WORK OUT

THEY'D BE DISCARDED JUST AS FREELY.

THE VERY SIGHT OF ONE WOULD DRIVE ALL THOUGHTS OF VANITY FROM HIS MIND.

25

JULIUS KNIPL
REAL ESTATE
PHOTOGRAPHER
3, VESEY ST.

GARDEN SPA
NCH · FOUNTAIN

IN THE TIME OF WOODROW WILSON, THEY WERE ALREADY ANCIENT MONUMENTS,

OLD, ALMOST BEYOND ANY OF THE AUTHENTIC TRADITIONS OF THAT PERIOD.

PLACED IN THE WINDOW BEHIND CARDBOARD AND CREPE PAPER DISPLAYS

WHERE NO HAND COULD EASILY REACH

THEY BECAME, OVER THE YEARS, COVERED WITH DUST AND DEAD INSECTS.

THE SIGHT OF THESE PLASTER OF PARIS ICE CREAMS WOULD REMIND MR. KNIPL OF THE COUNT-LESS SOULS WHO CAME BEFORE IN SEARCH OF A MOMENTARY PLEASURE

AND THIS THOUGHT GRADUALLY TAINTED HIS OWN ENJOYMENT OF REAL ICE CREAM.

WHY WERE THESE THINGS EVER MADE?

JUST SOMETHING TO PUT IN THE WINDOW

ONE OF MR. KNIPL'S FEW PLEASURES

IS NOW THE OBJECT OF AN ORGANIZED CAMPAIGN OF DENUNCIATION.

IN A SERIES OF EVENING LECTURES

THIS ZEALOT PRESENTS A CONVINCING ARGUMENT

AGAINST A SEEMINGLY INNOCENT HABIT.

WHAT GOES ON IN THESE CHEAP RESTAURANTS IS NOW A MATTER OF PUBLIC CONCERN.

THE CONSCIENCE OF THE CITY HOVERS ABOVE HIS HOT COFFEE.

THE SCAR OF A SIDE-WALK EXCAVATION TAKES YEARS TO COMPLETELY HEAL.

THE WORKERS LEAVE A WHITE PATCH

WITH INDELICATELY ETCHED EXPANSION LINES AND A NEW, SHARP CURB.

IN TIME, THROUGH THE GRATING OF SHOE LEATHER,

WEATHER AND HUMAN ACCIDENTS,

AND THE APPEARANCE OF THOSE MYSTERIOUS BLACK SPOTS,

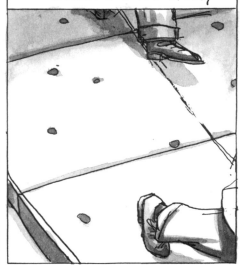

THE PATCH BEGINS TO BLEND IN WITH THE ADJOINING SIDEWALK

BUT, BECAUSE OF THE COMPOSITION OF NEW CONCRETE, IT WILL NEVER SPARKLE AT NIGHT.

WAS MR. KNIPL DREAMING

OR DID MEN ONCE WALK THE TRACKS OF THIS CITY'S SUBWAY SYSTEM?

THEY MUST HAVE BEEN HIRED TO INSPECT THE RAILS

BUT WERE ALWAYS READING FROM SOFT, LEATHER-BOUND BOOKS.

SUBWAY REGULATIONS OR THE HOLY BIBLE

MAYBE THIRTY YEARS AGO

NO, NEVER HEARD OF SUCH A THING

MR. KNIPL BEGINS TO WONDER

CHOCOLATE VENDING MACHINES

IF OTHER OF HIS FOND MEMORIES

SUBTERRANEAN LUNCHEONETTES

WERE OF AN IMAGINARY NATURE.

ADVERTISING PONIES

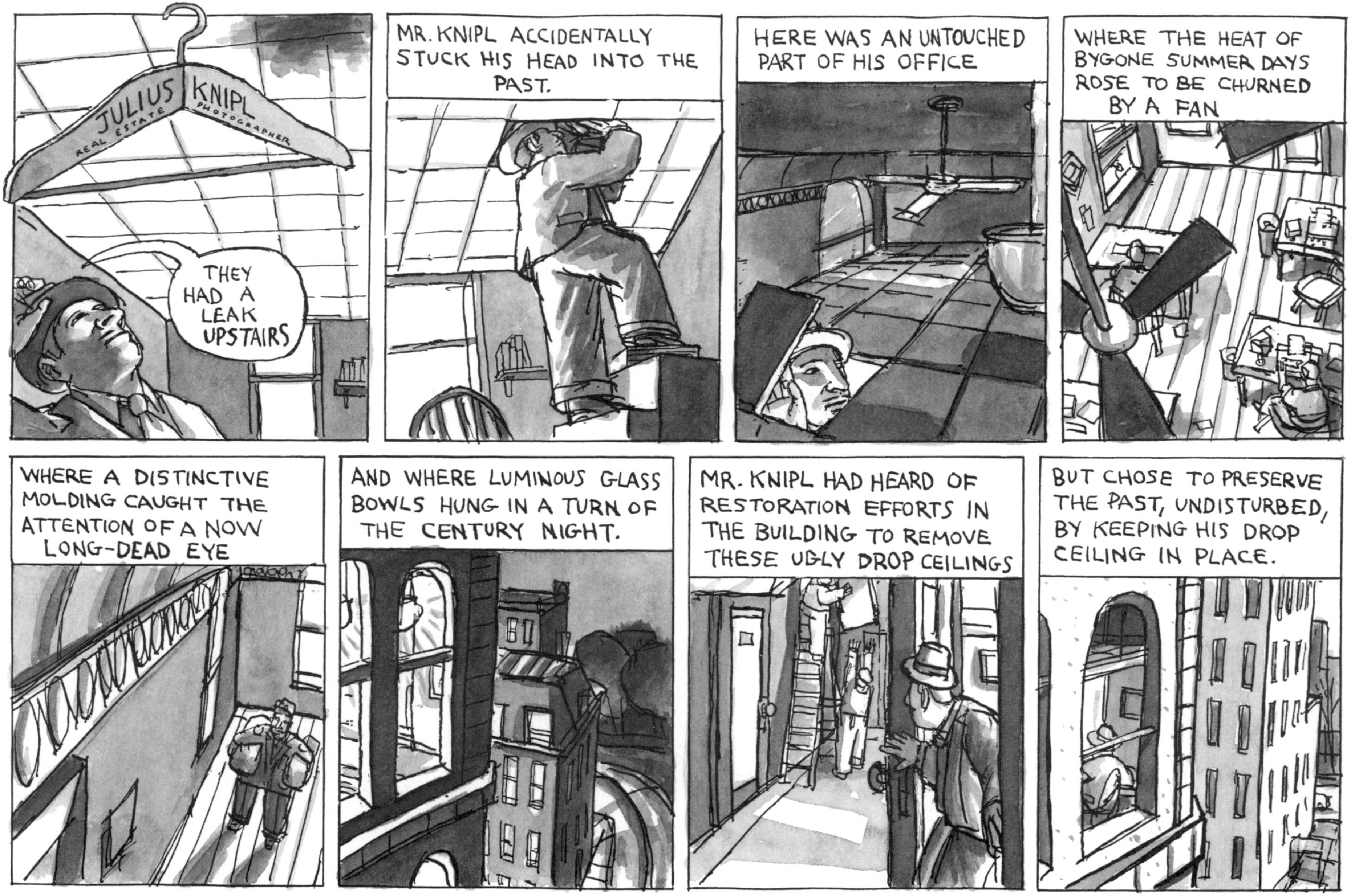
JULIUS KNIPL
REAL ESTATE PHOTOGRAPHER
THEY HAD A LEAK UPSTAIRS
MR. KNIPL ACCIDENTALLY STUCK HIS HEAD INTO THE PAST.
HERE WAS AN UNTOUCHED PART OF HIS OFFICE
WHERE THE HEAT OF BYGONE SUMMER DAYS ROSE TO BE CHURNED BY A FAN
WHERE A DISTINCTIVE MOLDING CAUGHT THE ATTENTION OF A NOW LONG-DEAD EYE
AND WHERE LUMINOUS GLASS BOWLS HUNG IN A TURN OF THE CENTURY NIGHT.
MR. KNIPL HAD HEARD OF RESTORATION EFFORTS IN THE BUILDING TO REMOVE THESE UGLY DROP CEILINGS
BUT CHOSE TO PRESERVE THE PAST, UNDISTURBED, BY KEEPING HIS DROP CEILING IN PLACE.

JULIUS KNIPL
REAL ESTATE PHOTOGRAPHER

HERE IT WAS — A TWO-STORY BUILDING ON MORTON AVENUE.

SO THIS IS WHERE IT'S IMPORTED

HOME OF PERU SAUCE

FISHBEIN FOODS

235

SHIPPING

BOTTLES OF PERU SAUCE HAD FOLLOWED MR. KNIPL INTO EVEN THE CHEAPEST RESTAURANTS OF THIS CITY,

ECONOMY RESTAURANT

OFFERING HIM A SENSE OF THE EXOTIC POSSIBILITIES EXISTING IN THIS WORLD.

PUNO BUTTER, CHICA, OCAS...

A GLANCE AT THE LABEL WITH ITS INGREDIENTS AND HIS PULSE WOULD QUICKEN.

SAUCE

16 FL

A DISGRUNTLED EMPLOYEE EXPLAINS —

NO. WE MAKE IT HERE. THE INGREDIENTS COME FROM NEW JERSEY.

SHIPPING

MR. FISHBEIN CAME BACK FROM MIAMI BEACH WITH THE IDEA. HIS BROTHER-IN-LAW'S A COMMERCIAL ARTIST.

WE MAKE ALL KINDS OF KETCHUPS AND HOT SAUCES, BUT PERU'S THE BIG SELLER.

FISHBEIN FOODS

235

PEOPLE SEEM TO LIKE IT.

PER

ALL HIS LIFE, MR. KNIPL HAS HEARD ACCOUNTS OF CELLAR DOOR INCIDENTS.

THE OTHER DAY...

THEY'D INVOLVE EITHER AN ERRANT YOUTH, RUSHING HOME AFTER HAVING COMMITTED SOME EXCESS,

OR A DISCONSOLATE MAN HOPING FOR SOMETHING TO HAPPEN.

THE DOORS ARE EITHER LEFT OPEN

OR COLLAPSE UNDER THE VICTIM'S WEIGHT;

HE'S EITHER TRAPPED FOR HOURS

PLEASE HELP!

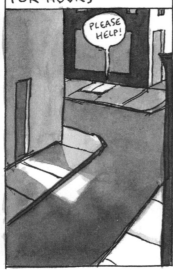

OR PERMANENTLY INJURED BY THE FALL.

THE CONCLUDING DETAILS ARE ALWAYS LACKING OR PURPOSELY AVOIDED.

I DON'T KNOW. THAT'S ALL I HEARD

IN THIS CITY, EACH CELLAR DOOR CONCEALS AN INEXPRESSIBLE MORAL.

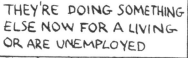 JULIUS KNIPL REAL ESTATE PHOTOGRAPHER

SOMEHOW, MR. KNIPL KNOWS.

THESE JOBS ARE NO LONGER THEIRS.

A CHAUFFEUR'S CAP

THEY'RE DOING SOMETHING ELSE NOW FOR A LIVING OR ARE UNEMPLOYED

FANCY WAITER'S PANTS

BUT CLING TO SOME REMNANT OF THEIR FORMER POSITION.

A COMPANY JACKET

HARKAVY PRODUCTIONS

HEAVY-DUTY SHOES

A SHIRT WITH AN EMBROIDERED NAME

Frank

EVEN MR. KNIPL SOMETIMES WEARS AN OLD PAIR OF THOSE SPECIALLY CUT TROUSERS FROM HIS DAYS AS A DANCE INSTRUCTOR.

WAY

33

"BOOK OF GREAT SECRETS AND VALUABLE MONEYMAKING RECIPES"

AT ONE TIME, THESE FORMULA BOOKS WERE BIG SELLERS.

PEOPLE LEARNED HOW TO MAKE THEIR OWN INK, CORN REMEDIES, COUGH MIXTURES, FURNITURE POLISH, HAIR DYE, ETC.

THE LOCAL CHEMISTS DEALT IN SMALL QUANTITIES OF ALL CHEMICALS.

AQUA FORTE - 2 OUNCES, POWDERED NUX VOMICA - 5 DROPS, ARMENIAN BOLE - 10 GRAINS, SYRUP MANNA - 2 DRACHMS

FENNEL WATER - 90 MINIMS, BRAN OF ALMONDS - ONE POUND

SUBTLE REFINEMENTS WERE MADE, BY INDIVIDUALS, UPON THE COMPOSITION OF TOOTH POWDER.

THE PREPARATION OF BLACK SHOE POLISH WAS AN ART.

MIX THE IVORY BLACK, SUGAR AND OLIVE OIL INTO A SMOOTH PASTE, ADDING THE BEER, A LITTLE AT A TIME, UNDER CONSTANT STIRRING. LET THIS STAND FOR 24 HOURS.

SEVERAL WELL-KNOWN COMPANIES WERE STARTED WITH A FEW DOLLARS WORTH OF GUM ARABIC.

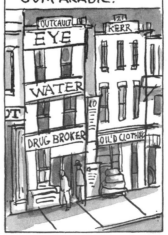

TODAY, SUCH CONCOCTIONS WOULD BE CONSIDERED DANGEROUS FRAUDS.

MY EYES ARE KILLING ME!

COMFORT AND RELIEF ARE FOUND ONLY IN SIGHT OF A REGISTERED TRADEMARK.

A PHONE BOOTH'S LOCATION EXERTS A SUBTLE INFLUENCE ON THE PERSON USING IT.

THE CALLER'S THOUGHTS AND CHOICE OF WORDS REFLECT THE IMMEDIATE LANDSCAPE.

A WINDY CORNER NEXT TO A FOREIGN RESTAURANT.

UH... COULD BE... WE SEE... WHA MEANS? ...EH?... NO LIKE IT... HELLO?... OK...

IN THE WARM LIGHT OF AN ALL-NIGHT BAKERY.

FOR YOU?! NO PROBLEM! I'M WITH YOU A HUNDRED PERCENT. WE'RE OLD FRIENDS... RIGHT? WOULD I MAKE YOU BUY A PICTURE YOU'RE NOT CRAZY ABOUT? ...WOULD I! NAAAH.

ON A DESERTED HIGHWAY

WHAT'S THE POINT?...... ...THEY'RE OF NO USE TO YOU WHATSOEVER... ...THIS BUSINESS CAN'T GO ON INDEFINITELY ...I CAN'T TALK NOW... IT'S NO USE...

A BUSY INDUSTRIAL AREA

CUT THE CRAP! LOOK IT, YA WANT THE GODDAMN PICTURES? IT'S NO SKIN OFF MY BACK!... WHATTA YA TALKIN'?... THAT'S BULLSHIT!

FOR THIS REASON, YOU CAN'T ALWAYS RECOGNIZE THE LITTLE VOICE YOU HEAR ON THE PHONE.

WHO IS THIS?! IT'S ME— KNIPL!

35

MR. KNIPL RETURNS A RENTED TUXEDO.

I DON'T FEEL WELL

THE OWNER EXAMINES IT FOR DAMAGES...

WHAT AN AFFAIR! YOU HAVE NO IDEA!... UNTIL TWO O'CLOCK IN THE MORNING!

EMPTIES THE POCKETS OF INVITATIONS, CARNATIONS AND YARMULKES.

SO MUCH TO EAT! I'M STILL SICK!

THE MANIKINS WERE LAST DRESSED IN 1961.

AND MY LEGS! FROM THE DANCING

HMM. A 40 SHORT.

MR. KNIPL'S SIZE REMINDS THE OWNER

YOU KNOW, IT'S HAPPENED ON SEVERAL OCCASIONS...

I HAD TO GO DOWN TO CLAIM A TUX AT THE HOSPITAL MORGUE

YEAH, THAT'S IT. A 40 SHORT

TOO MUCH DRINKING, FOOD, DANCING, TOO MUCH.

YOU SEE! IT PAYS TO RENT.

STEP UP TO BARGAINS

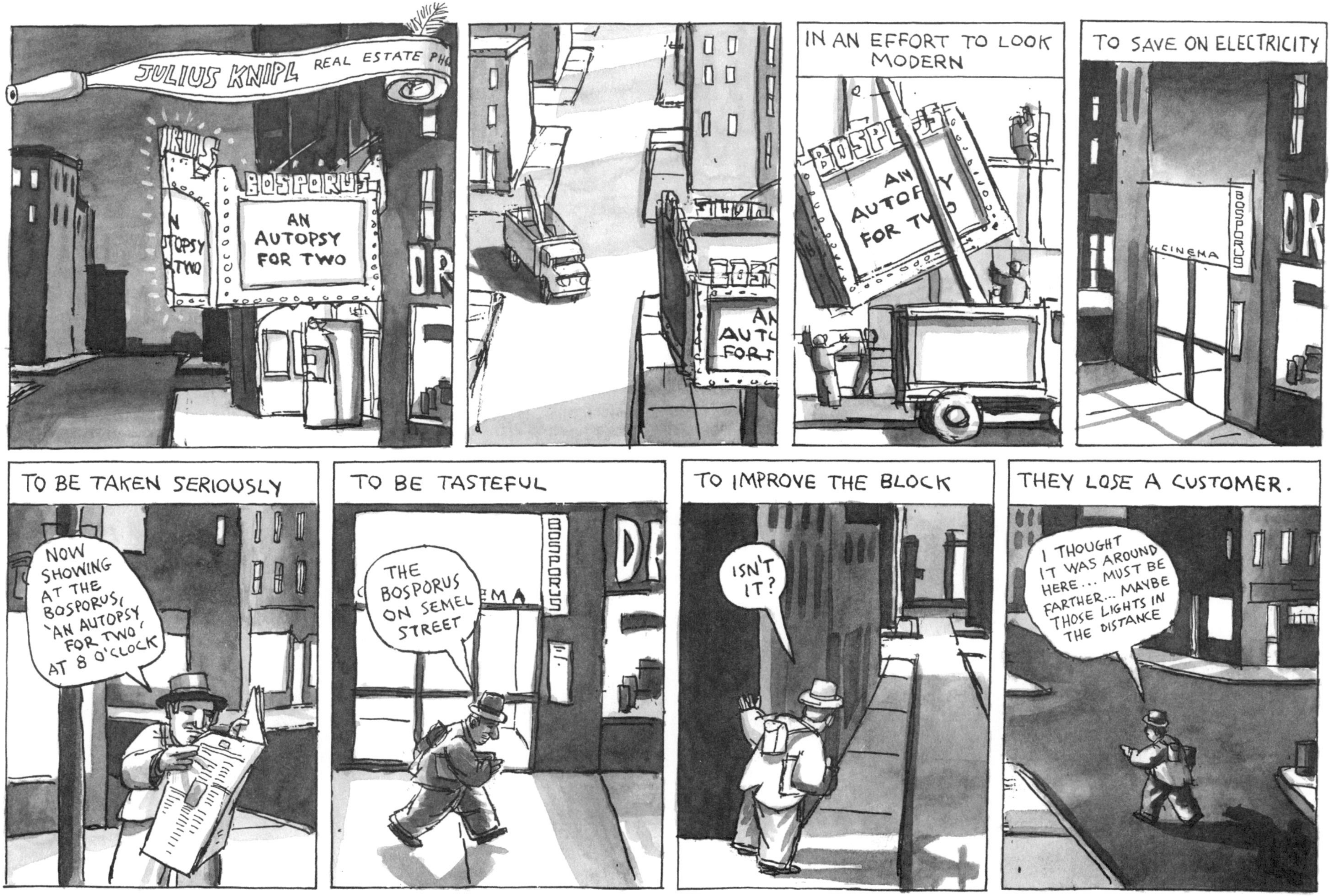
JULIUS KNIPL REAL ESTATE PHO
BOSPORUS
AN AUTOPSY FOR TWO
IN AN EFFORT TO LOOK MODERN
TO SAVE ON ELECTRICITY
CINEMA
BOSPORUS
TO BE TAKEN SERIOUSLY
NOW SHOWING AT THE BOSPORUS, 'AN AUTOPSY FOR TWO' AT 8 O'CLOCK
TO BE TASTEFUL
BOSPORUS
THE BOSPORUS ON SEMEL STREET
TO IMPROVE THE BLOCK
ISN'T IT?
THEY LOSE A CUSTOMER.
I THOUGHT IT WAS AROUND HERE... MUST BE FARTHER... MAYBE THOSE LIGHTS IN THE DISTANCE

MR. KNIPL SAW THIS SIGN

FROM A DISTANCE,

ON HIS WAY SOMEWHERE ELSE,

EVERY DAY, FOR YEARS.

ONE DAY, HE WENT TO LOOK FOR A LIGHTWEIGHT JACKET.

THAT'S THE LOCATION

I'M VERY EXCITED. I BOUGHT TWO STACKED OVENS

I PLAN TO SERVE SLICES—BOTH REGULAR AND SICILIAN—AND HAVE A SPECIAL MENU WITH HEROES—EGGPLANT PARMIGIANA, MEATBALL AND VEAL. I DON'T WANNA GET INTO SPAGHETTI.

OVER THE YEARS, MR. KNIPL HAD WALKED PAST AND LOOKED INTO HUNDREDS OF PIZZA PLACES

SIMILAR TO THE ONE ENVISIONED BY THIS MAN.

A MERCIFUL LAPSE OF MEMORY OCCURS DURING THE ACT OF CONCEPTION

THIS IS MY IDEA. A COUNTER WITH A GLASS HOOD TO DISPLAY THE HOT PIES

WHICH ALLOWS A MAN TO BECOME EXCITED

THEN ANOTHER COUNTER, OPPOSITE, FOR PEOPLE TO STAND AND EAT. WHATTA YA THINK?

EVEN BY THE IDEA OF OPENING A NEW PIZZA PLACE.

I'D LIKE ONE OR TWO TABLES IN THE BACK, BEHIND THE SODA CASE, AND ON THE WALL A PAINTING OF THE BAY OF NAPLES.

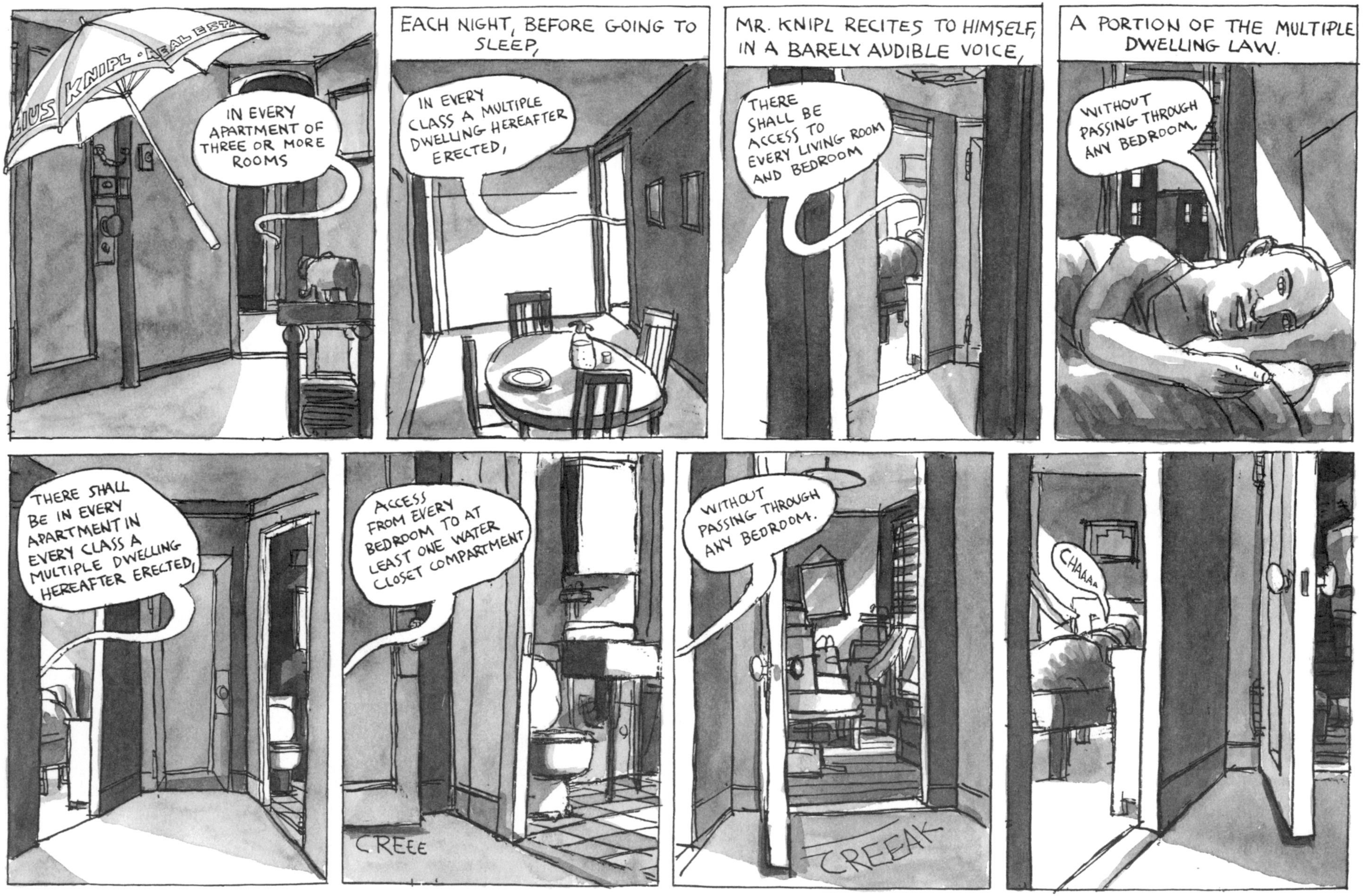

LIUS KNIPL • REAL ESTA
IN EVERY APARTMENT OF THREE OR MORE ROOMS
EACH NIGHT, BEFORE GOING TO SLEEP,
IN EVERY CLASS A MULTIPLE DWELLING HEREAFTER ERECTED,
MR. KNIPL RECITES TO HIMSELF, IN A BARELY AUDIBLE VOICE,
THERE SHALL BE ACCESS TO EVERY LIVING ROOM AND BEDROOM
A PORTION OF THE MULTIPLE DWELLING LAW.
WITHOUT PASSING THROUGH ANY BEDROOM.
THERE SHALL BE IN EVERY APARTMENT IN EVERY CLASS A MULTIPLE DWELLING HEREAFTER ERECTED,
ACCESS FROM EVERY BEDROOM TO AT LEAST ONE WATER CLOSET COMPARTMENT
CREEE
WITHOUT PASSING THROUGH ANY BEDROOM.
CREEAK
CHAAAA

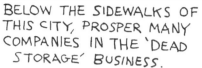

ALL MY NEGATIVES FROM 1961

BELOW THE SIDEWALKS OF THIS CITY, PROSPER MANY COMPANIES IN THE 'DEAD STORAGE' BUSINESS.

IS THIS STORAGE IN PERPETUITY OR JUST FOR YOUR LIFETIME?

SAY THIRTY YEARS

YOU HAVE NO INTENTION OF WANTING TO EXAMINE THIS MATERIAL FOR THE NEXT THIRTY YEARS?

I DOUBT IT.

YOU HAVE NOTHING HERE OF ANY VALUE WHATSOEVER TO ANYONE BUT YOURSELF?

BELIEVE ME, IT'S NOTHING

YOU ACCEPT THE LIKELIHOOD OF WATER, SEWER AND VERMIN DAMAGES TO THE MATERIALS HEREIN CONTAINED?

IF IT HAPPENS, IT HAPPENS.

FINE. MY NAME IS JULIUS KN...

THE NAME'S NOT NECESSARY

ALL PAYMENT IS IN ADVANCE. $2 PER YEAR.

THAT'S ONE ADDRESS I CAN FORGET.

IN THE PAST, MR. KNIPL HAD BEEN FORCED, BY CIRCUMSTANCES, TO WATCH

THIS PUBLIC DISPLAY OF A MAN'S NEED FOR CHEAP CARBOHYDRATES,

POOR GUY.

FROM THE CORNER OF HIS EYE, HE SAW WHITE ISLANDS FORM IN A CUP OF BLACK COFFEE.

THE COMMUNAL SUGAR DISPENSER HAS BEEN REPLACED BY AN INHERENTLY CRUEL INVENTION —

HOW MANY SUGARS?

THE INDIVIDUAL PACKET OF SUGAR.

LONG AFTER THE CONTENTS HAVE DISSOLVED,

THE TORN PACKETS BEAR WITNESS TO THE SAME DESPERATE ACT.

THE PROGRESSIVE LAUNDRY

MR. KNIPL FINDS COMFORT

THEY REALLY KNEW HOW TO BUILD 'EM

IN THE SIGHT OF AN ARCHITECTURAL REMNANT

MUST HAVE COST A FORTUNE

OF SOME GREAT COMMERCIAL VENTURE

IN THOSE DAYS, PEOPLE THOUGHT BIG

FUNERAL HOME

WHICH STANDS

NONE OF THIS FLIMSY CONSTRUCTION

USELESS AND ABANDONED

THEY MEANT BUSINESS

IN THIS PART OF THE CITY

IT'S A LANDMARK

BECAUSE NO ONE CAN AFFORD TO DEMOLISH IT.

YOU CAN SEE IT TWENTY BLOCKS AWAY.

43

IN THIS NEIGHBORHOOD, LARGE NUMBERS OF MEN ARE PUT TO WORK POLISHING DOORKNOBS AND DOCTORS' PLAQUES.

IT'S A STRANGELY FAMILIAR SHINE

DUE TO REPEATED RUBBING OVER A LONG PERIOD OF TIME.

A SIGN OF PERMANENCE AND RELIABILITY

MR. KNIPL NOTICES THE SAME SHINE ON THE SEAT OF TAXI DRIVERS' PANTS,

ON BALD HEADS

AND SUBWAY BANISTERS.

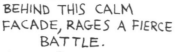

Panel 1:
JULIUS KNIPL
Real estate photographer
SHUCKEL'S FOUNTAIN · CANDY
ICE CREAM

Panel 2:
BEHIND THIS CALM FACADE, RAGES A FIERCE BATTLE.
HELLO, AM I SPEAKING...

Panel 3:
SALESMEN FROM COMPETING CIGAR COMPANIES GO AFTER THE SAME CANDY STORE.
WITH THE PROPRIETOR?

Panel 4:
ONE HAS AN EGYPTIAN NAME,
HOTEP-RA CIGARS
FINE CIGARS
HOTEP-RA
DIRECT FROM EGYPT
MR. SHUCKEL, IT COSTS YOU NOTHING

Panel 5:
THE OTHER, SPANISH.
Gamba y Castro CIGARS
ICE CREAM
THE BEST CIGAR
IMPORTE
GAMBA Y CASTRO
JUST GIVE ME THE OK AND WE SET YOU UP NICE

Panel 6:
THEY BOTH OFFER A BEAUTIFUL SIGN, WINDOW DISPLAYS AND DISCOUNTS.
I CAN SHOW YOU

Panel 7:
THE CANDY STORE OWNER'S WIFE, WHO HATES THE SMELL OF CIGARS,
TELEPHONE
WE HAVE STORES ALL OVER THE CITY

Panel 8:
SIGNS AN AGREEMENT WITH THE AGENT FROM A FAMOUS SODA COMPANY.
SHUCKEL FOUNTAIN CANDY
ICE CREAM
DRINK Grapz

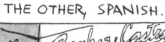

45

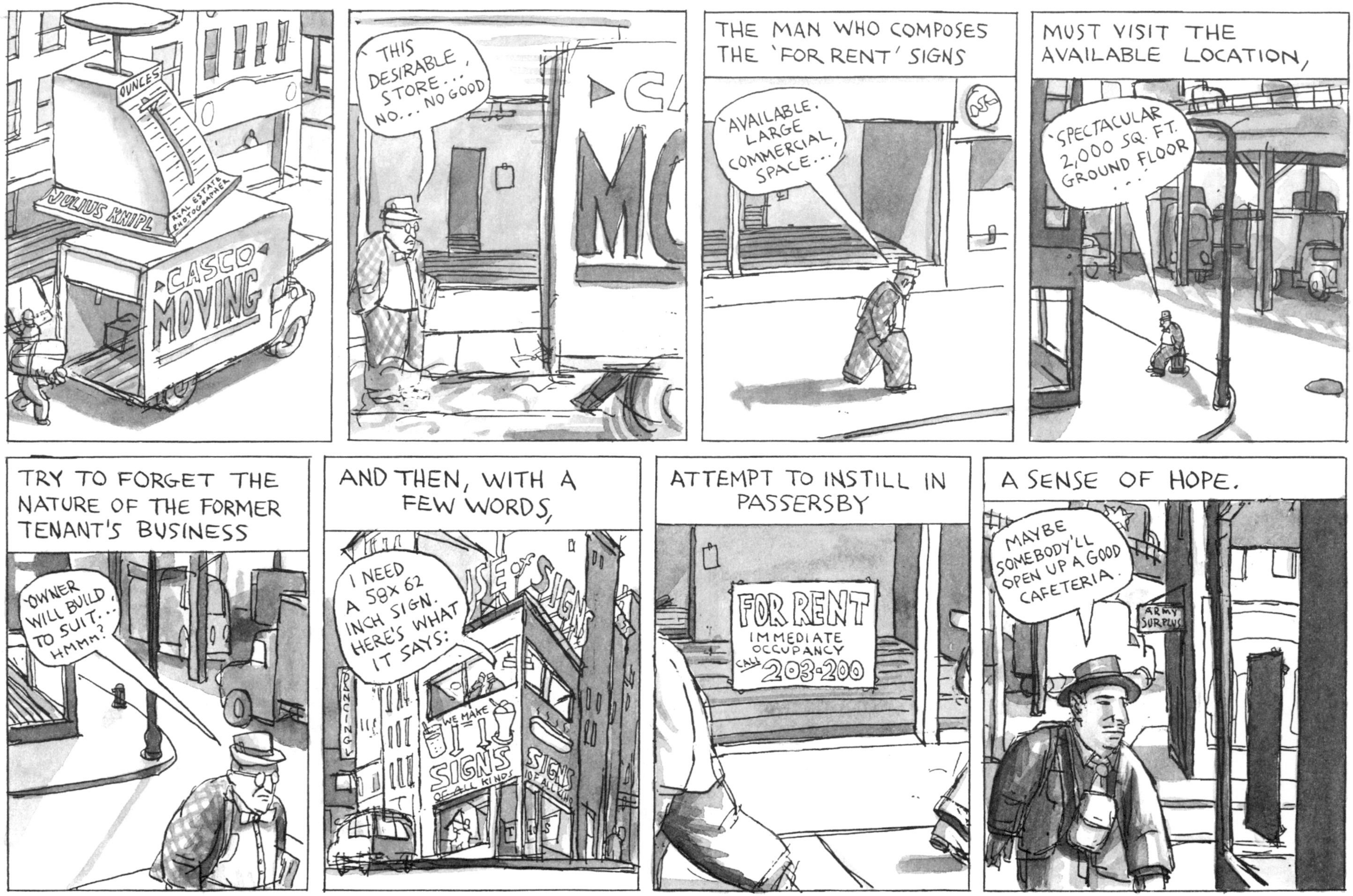
THIS DESIRABLE STORE... NO... NO GOOD
THE MAN WHO COMPOSES THE 'FOR RENT' SIGNS
AVAILABLE. LARGE COMMERCIAL SPACE...
MUST VISIT THE AVAILABLE LOCATION,
SPECTACULAR 2,000 SQ. FT. GROUND FLOOR...
TRY TO FORGET THE NATURE OF THE FORMER TENANT'S BUSINESS
OWNER WILL BUILD TO SUIT... HMMM?
AND THEN, WITH A FEW WORDS,
I NEED A 58x62 INCH SIGN. HERE'S WHAT IT SAYS:
ATTEMPT TO INSTILL IN PASSERSBY
FOR RENT
IMMEDIATE OCCUPANCY
CALL 203-200
A SENSE OF HOPE.
MAYBE SOMEBODY'LL OPEN UP A GOOD CAFETERIA.

ONE DOCTOR LURKS AROUND LATE AT NIGHT.

HE KEEPS FUNNY OFFICE HOURS

HE HAS TO

FOR YEARS, HIS KIND OF PRACTICE WASN'T EXACTLY KOSHER YOU KNOW... WHEN A WOMAN GOT IN TROUBLE... NEEDED HELP

OR A FELLA COMMITTED A LITTLE INDISCRETION AND COULDN'T TALK TO HIS REGULAR DOCTOR

AND THEN THERE'S ALL KINDS OF WORK MOST DOCTORS WOULDN'T TOUCH

YOU KNOW... TATTOO REMOVAL, 'ACCIDENTAL' GUNSHOT WOUNDS, CHORUS-GIRL ITCH, GAMBLER'S CRAMPS...

OR PEOPLE NEED CERTAIN 'PRESCRIPTIONS' NO REGULAR DOCTOR WOULD WRITE.

'CLICK'

MOST OF THOSE PROCEDURES ARE PERFECTLY LEGAL NOW. I'M SURPRISED HE STILL HAS BUSINESS.

OH, JESUS! THAT'S A NEW ONE ON ME... BUT SURE, COME IN... I CAN FIX YOU UP.

TEN O'CLOCK. NO WONDER I'M HUNGRY.

IT'S DONE TO WASH THE FLOORS AT NIGHT

BUT TO MR. KNIPL, IT'S A SIGN,

A SANDWICH AT THE UNION DELICATESSEN. THEY'RE OPEN LATE.

VISIBLE ACROSS A BUSY STREET

AND INSTANTLY UNDERSTOOD TO MEAN

I LIKE A GOOD SOUR TOMATO

THAT IT'S TOO LATE

THE LIGHT'S ON

FOR A BRISKET OF BEEF SANDWICH.

A MEAT LOAF PLATE AT THE NATIONAL CAFETERIA

WHAT'S THIS?

THE EIGHT OF CLUBS FROM A DECK OF LAMINATED PLAYING CARDS

WITH A PHOTO OF A NAKED WOMAN ON THE BACK.

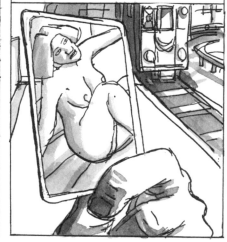

A POPULAR ITEM, BOUGHT IN A NOVELTY STORE NEXT DOOR TO A FAMOUS BOXING ARENA

CARRIED FOR MONTHS IN THE POCKET OF A REVERSIBLE JACKET

IDLY SHUFFLED IN PRIVATE

HAVING NO OPPORTUNITY TO BE USED SOCIALLY

THEN, SUDDENLY RENDERED USELESS

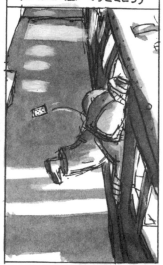

BY THE LOSS OF ONE CARD.

I HATE TO SEE A DECK OF CARDS RUINED

THE SOUND OF A LARGE FLAG IN THE DARK

LIKE WAVES AGAINST A DISTANT SHORE

MR. KNIPL IMAGINES THE EMBLEM OF THIS FOREIGN NATION

DISPLAYED EVERYWHERE— BUT WITH DISCRETION

ON SECOND STORY RESTAURANT WINDOWS

ON THE LAPELS OF LAME MEN

ON CHEAPLY PRINTED PAMPHLETS

AND IN SUGAR ON SMALL CAKES.

IN THE MORNING HE CAN SEE.

TRY A GRAPE BOSPHORUS. IT'S THE NEWEST THING

AS ONE SODA FOUNTAIN DRINK WAS BORN

IT'S SELTZER, GRAPE SYRUP AND MALTED MILK

LEMME HAVE A LARGE

ANOTHER WOULD FADE INTO OBLIVION.

I'D LIKE A COLD HERBERT WATER

WHO?

WHAT WERE COMMON NAMES,

A CHERRY LAKE... A NORMONA... A LATIN CREAM ...A NADJY... A VANILLA TYROL...

ARE SUDDENLY ARCHAIC TERMS IN THE MOUTHS OF OLD MEN.

A HERBERT WATER

NEVER HEARD OF IT

FOR TWENTY-FIVE YEARS, AT BEST,

I JUST HAD ONE TEN YEARS AGO

CAN A CERTAIN COMBINATION OF CARBONATED WATER,

WITH SELTZER TO THE TOP

NO

SYRUP

THEN A LITTLE ROSE SYRUP

NO

AND THAT UNLIKELY THIRD INGREDIENT

HALF SOUR MILK

THE FOUNTAIN'S BROKEN

COMMAND THE PALATE OF A FICKLE PUBLIC.

ALL WE HAVE ARE CANS

KOZMA LUNCHEONETTE

A SMALL BUSINESS WOULD THRIVE JUST BECAUSE OF ITS PROXIMITY TO THE PLACE.

IT WAS A LANDMARK

KNOWN BY NAME THROUGH-OUT THE CITY.

NOW, IT IS A PAINFULLY STRANGE APPELLATION

EVERYONE WANTED TO CASH IN ON THAT NAME

BEFITTING A RIVER IN EASTERN EUROPE OR A PATENTED COFFEE SUBSTITUTE.

I REMEMBER THE KOZMA

A BIG THEATER, ON THAT CORNER

THEY KNOCKED IT DOWN SIX YEARS AGO.

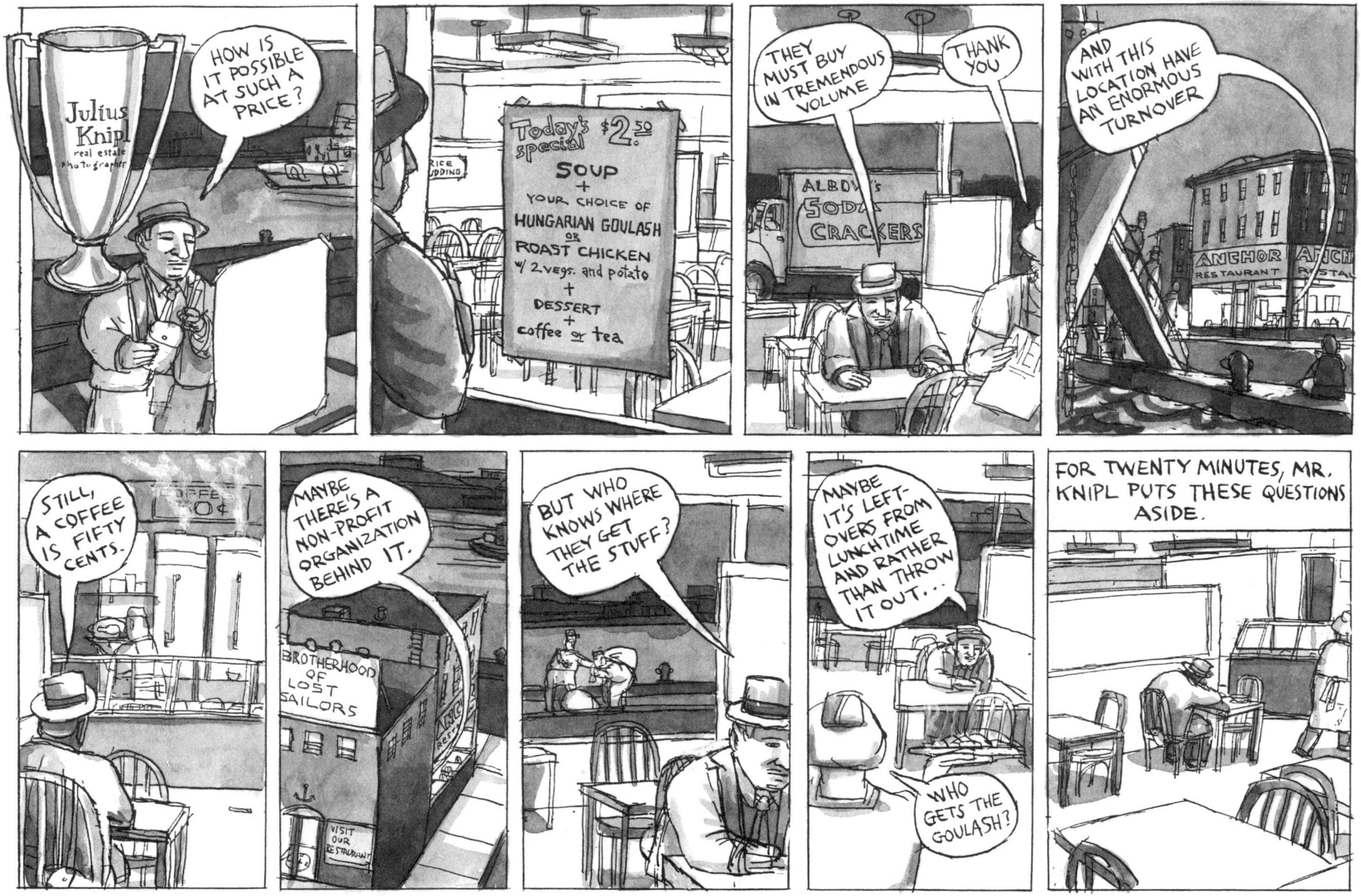
Julius Knipl real estate photographer
HOW IS IT POSSIBLE AT SUCH A PRICE?
Today's special $2.50
SOUP + YOUR CHOICE OF HUNGARIAN GOULASH OR ROAST CHICKEN w/ 2 vegs. and potato + DESSERT + coffee or tea
THEY MUST BUY IN TREMENDOUS VOLUME
THANK YOU
AND WITH THIS LOCATION HAVE AN ENORMOUS TURNOVER
ANCHOR RESTAURANT
STILL, A COFFEE IS FIFTY CENTS.
MAYBE THERE'S A NON-PROFIT ORGANIZATION BEHIND IT.
BROTHERHOOD OF LOST SAILORS
VISIT OUR RESTAURANT
BUT WHO KNOWS WHERE THEY GET THE STUFF?
MAYBE IT'S LEFT-OVERS FROM LUNCHTIME AND RATHER THAN THROW IT OUT...
WHO GETS THE GOULASH?
FOR TWENTY MINUTES, MR. KNIPL PUTS THESE QUESTIONS ASIDE.

JULIUS KNIPL
real estate
photographer

3/4
1/2
1/4

THEY LIKE TO STAND

MR. KNIPL KNOWS WHERE ALL THE LONG DISTANCE BUS DRIVERS GO FOR COFFEE.

TWO ...THREE HUNDRED MILES MEAN NOTHING TO THESE MEN

YOU'LL HAVE FOG ALL THE WAY FROM THE BRIDGE TO OLDMAN STATE PARK...

THEN JUST BEYOND THE FALLING ROCK ZONE ON ROUTE SEVEN...

THERE'S A DETOUR

THAT'LL TAKE YOU THROUGH POLIOVILLE.

YOU PASS A BIG CHRISTMAS TREE FARM

AND THEN NOTHING FOR TEN MILES UNTIL YOU COME TO A WORLD WAR ONE MONUMENT.

THE PLACE IS JUST OPPOSITE ON YOUR RIGHT.

PETE'S
DRINKS
HOT COLD
FRESH
WARM
STOP HERE!
YOU BET IT'S

WITHOUT LEAVING THE CITY, MR. KNIPL FEELS A PANG OF HOMESICKNESS.

IT'S THE BEST COFFEE IN THE STATE!

IN THESE CUT-RATE CLOTHING STORES, OPEN TO THE STREET, THEFT IS COMMON.

ONE OWNER GOT AN IDEA WHILE LYING ON THE BEACH.

HIRE HEALTHY YOUNG MEN TO SIT IN THE SUN AND WATCH

JUST LIKE ON THE BEACH.

ONLY IF THESE GUARDS GET TO A PERSON IN TIME

THE GREEN JACKET

THAT PERSON DROWNS.

SAVE-A-LOT CLOTHING VS. ROMAN OUZEL

WE TRUST

THIS PEEPHOLE WAS SMEARED WHEN I MOVED IN

IN HIS APARTMENT, MR. KNIPL DISCOVERS TRACES OF A PREVIOUS TENANT.

SOMEONE WHO HAD A TABLE HERE

WHO HAD A LOT OF PICTURES TO HANG

WHO SPOILED THE DOORKNOBS WITH A SWEATY HAND

PUT PIECES OF BLACK MASKING TAPE UNDER ALL THE CABINETS

RUBBED AWAY THE BATHTUB'S PORCELAIN FINISH

SHARPENED KNIVES ON THE WINDOW SILL

AND WORE THIS LIGHT SWITCH TO A NUB

A RETIRED CARPET SALESMAN'S UNINTENTIONALLY CONSTRUCTED MEMORIAL TO HIMSELF.

SURE I REMEMBER. BEFORE YOU WAS AN OLD MAN NAMED ROTMAN.

ON RAINY DAYS, A RUBBER BAND SALESMAN CANVASSES MR. KNIPL'S BUILDING.

A COUPLE OF THESE

HIS SLEEVES AND TROUSER LEGS HELD FIRMLY BY #4S.

NEED ANY RUBBER BANDS?

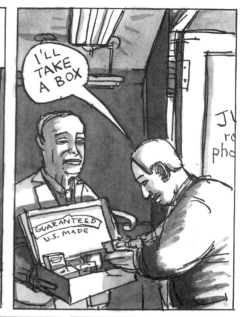

I'LL TAKE A BOX

HE'S ONLY MOTIVATED TO GO OUT AND SELL ON LOUSY DAYS.

IT'S THE SOUND OF RAIN ON THE WINDOW OF HIS FURNISHED ROOM

THE IDEA OF A PUDDLE FORMING IN HIS EMPTY BANK ACCOUNT

AND THE SIGHT OF A BACKED UP SEWER

THAT REMIND HIM OF HIS UNSOLD STOCK OF ASSORTED RUBBER BANDS.

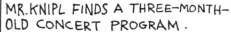

MR. KNIPL FINDS A THREE-MONTH-OLD CONCERT PROGRAM.

DECEMBER 19th, AT 8 P.M.

SOMETHING HE'D NEVER HEARD OF, AT A HALL HE KNOWS ONLY BY NAME.

HARRY JOIST PLAYS THE POSTHUMOUS WORKS OF CARLO MACAROON.

A MIDDLE-AGED MAN WAS TO ATTEMPT TO PLAY THE WORK OF A RECENTLY DECEASED COMPOSER ON A DIFFICULT ETHNIC INSTRUMENT.

IT WAS A WINTER EVENING, FULL OF CULTURAL EVENTS.

HURRY. IT'S ALMOST EIGHT

WHAT WAS I DOING THAT NIGHT?

A MIDDLE-AGED MAN, CARRYING AN ODDLY SHAPED INSTRUMENT CASE, LEFT THE TOLSTOY VEGETARIAN RESTAURANT

OH, YEAH

HIS SUIT ALREADY STAINED WITH EGG AND TOMATO.

I REMEMBER

THAT'S IMPOSSIBLE TO READ.

ON THESE OLDER BUILDINGS, MR. KNIPL HAS SEEN LETTERED WINDOWS UP AS HIGH AS THE TWENTIETH FLOOR.

COULD IT BE THAT PEOPLE ONCE HAD MORE ACUTE EYESIGHT?

FORTY YEARS AGO, A CERTAIN UNSCRUPULOUS SIGN PAINTER BEGAN TO SOLICIT WORK DOOR TO DOOR

COMPANIES LOCATED ON HIGHER FLOORS HAD NEVER CONSIDERED A WINDOW SIGN

I JUST DID MANDALAY FABRICS DOWN-STAIRS...

BUT, UPON LEARNING THAT THE PEOPLE DOWNSTAIRS HAD THEIR WINDOWS LETTERED,

...BEING IN THE BUILDING, I CAN GIVE YOU A GOOD PRICE.

FIGURED THAT ONE MORE FLOOR COULDN'T MAKE MUCH DIFFERENCE IN LEGIBILITY

IT LOOKS BETTER FROM THE OUTSIDE.

AND SO DECIDED TO TAKE ADVANTAGE OF THIS INEXPEN-SIVE FORM OF ADVERTISING.

19th FLOOR, THIRD WINDOW FROM THE END... HMM?

BEARSKIN COMPANY! BEARSKIN COMPANY! I'M TELLING YOU THAT'S WHAT IT SAYS!

AFTER FINISHING A JOB, THE SIGN PAINTER WOULD MOVE ON TO A STILL HIGHER FLOOR.

JULIUS KNIPL
REAL ESTATE
PHOTOGRAPHER

ONE EVEN

PERFECT, LARGE-SCALE REPRODUCTIONS OF U.S. ONE HUNDRED DOLLAR BILLS.

ONE OUTTA FIVE

PRICE: ONE DOLLAR

I'LL TAKE ONE

ONE OUTTA TEN

GAMBLING DOGS AND RELIGIOUS SCENES NEVER SELL AS WELL.

STOREKEEPERS BUY THESE JUMBO BILLS TO HANG OVER A CASH REGISTER.

BUT MOST PEOPLE JUST TAKE THEM HOME TO LOOK AT.

HE STUFFS THE FIVES AND TENS INTO ONE POCKET, THE SINGLES COME OUT OF ANOTHER.

ONE OUTTA FIVE

AT THE END OF THE DAY, HE UNWRINKLES HIS EARNINGS...

LET'S SEE...

HAMMERST
DAIRY

ONE OUT OF A GROWING NUMBER OF PEOPLE WHO APPRECIATE MONEY FOR ITS PURELY DECORATIVE QUALITIES.

NOODLES AND CHEESE AND A COFFEE? THAT'S $3.50.

THERE'S A LITTLE HAND, REACHING DOWN BEHIND YOU,

BY WHAT SUBTLE FORM OF INCULCATION

IN THE DARKEST NIGHT, WHERE THERE IS NO LIGHT.

DO THE WORDS AND MELODY OF A POPULAR SONG

PUT 'ER THERE MY FRIEND, PUT 'ER THERE OLD STRANGER

ENTER THE SUBCONSCIOUS MIND OF A BUSY MAN.

LITTLE HAND FROM NOWHERE, LITTLE HAND OF TIME.

A TV VARIETY SHOW HEARD THROUGH A WALL.

AND THIS LITTLE HAND, REACHING DOWN BEHIND YOU,

FROM THE RADIO OF A PASSING CAR

SCRATCHES WHERE IT ITCHES, IN THE DARK OF NIGHT.

THROUGH SUCH EFFORTLESS ASSIMILATION, A BUSY MAN MAY NOT EVEN REALIZE WHAT IT IS THAT HE'S LEARNT

PUT 'ER THERE MY FRIEND, PUT 'ER THERE OLD STRANGER

QUIET.

FROM AN OPEN WINDOW AT DUSK.

LITTLE HAND FROM NOWHERE, LITTLE HAND OF TIME.

61

AT ABOUT 10 A.M. THERE IS A LULL IN THE DAY'S COMMERCIAL ACTIVITY.

BUSINESSMEN STOP AND GO OUT FOR COFFEE.

REFLECTED IN THE GLAZE OF A CHEESE DANISH

ARE A SUCCESSION OF STOOPED FIGURES.

A LIGHT COFFEE AND A CHEESE DANISH

IF ONE OF THESE MEN HAPPENED TO LOOK IN THE RIGHT DIRECTION, HE'D SEE A MINIATURE IMAGE OF HIMSELF

A BLACK COFFEE AND A CHEESE DANISH

BATHED IN THAT GOLDEN LIGHT THAT EMANATES FROM THE SOURCE OF ALL BENEVOLENT COMMERCIAL KNOWLEDGE

TWO REGULARS AND TWO CHEESE DANISH

IN THIS CASE, A MECHANICALLY APPLIED MIXTURE OF EGG AND WATER BAKED TO A THIN, GLISTENING CRUST.

A REGULAR COFFEE AND A CHEESE DANISH.

ALL OUT OF CHEESE DANISH, HOW ABOUT A LINZER TART?

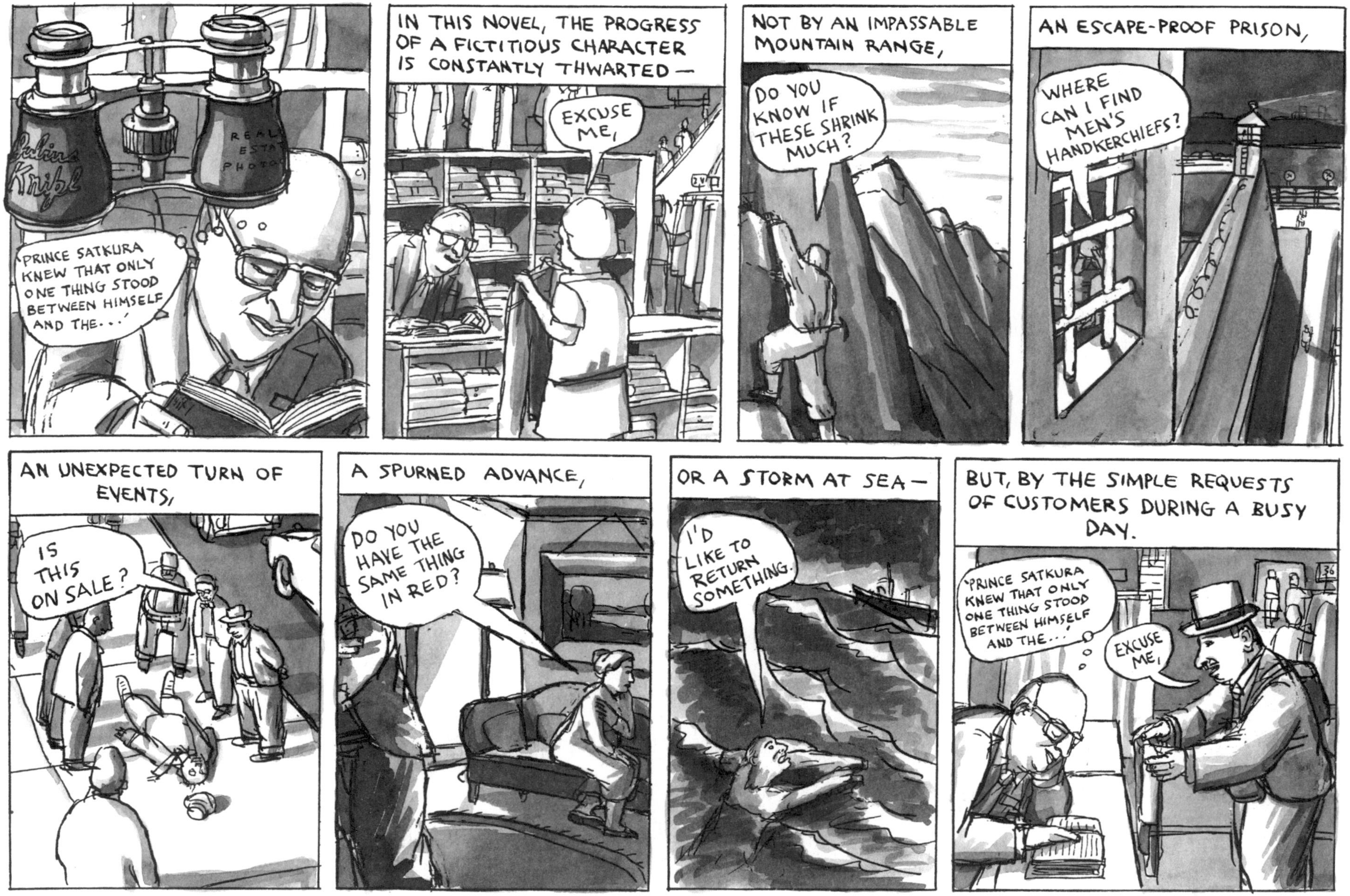

'PRINCE SATKURA KNEW THAT ONLY ONE THING STOOD BETWEEN HIMSELF AND THE...'
IN THIS NOVEL, THE PROGRESS OF A FICTITIOUS CHARACTER IS CONSTANTLY THWARTED—
EXCUSE ME,
NOT BY AN IMPASSABLE MOUNTAIN RANGE,
DO YOU KNOW IF THESE SHRINK MUCH?
AN ESCAPE-PROOF PRISON,
WHERE CAN I FIND MEN'S HANDKERCHIEFS?
AN UNEXPECTED TURN OF EVENTS,
IS THIS ON SALE?
A SPURNED ADVANCE,
DO YOU HAVE THE SAME THING IN RED?
OR A STORM AT SEA—
I'D LIKE TO RETURN SOMETHING.
BUT, BY THE SIMPLE REQUESTS OF CUSTOMERS DURING A BUSY DAY.
'PRINCE SATKURA KNEW THAT ONLY ONE THING STOOD BETWEEN HIMSELF AND THE...'
EXCUSE ME,

JULIUS KNIPL
REAL ESTATE
PHOTOGRAPHER

I RENT A STORE ON A BUSY STREET...

MR. KNIPL MEETS A MAN IN THE 'GOING OUT OF BUSINESS' TRADE.

AND FILL IT WITH ALL KINDS OF CAMERAS AND ELECTRONIC ITEMS.

REGULAR PRICES... NO BARGAINS. MAYBE A COUPLE TOURISTS WANDER IN. THEN, AFTER A FEW WEEKS...

I GO OUT OF BUSINESS! SIGNS, LOUDSPEAKERS, HANDBILLS! 'EVERYTHING MUST GO!'

PEOPLE CAN'T RESIST IT.

MY LAST STORE WENT OUT OF BUSINESS FOR THREE YEARS.

YES! YES! YES!

BY THAT TIME, EVERY-ONE'S SEEN IT, IT'S PLAYED OUT AND YOU CAN CLOSE UP QUIETLY, FOR REAL.

I WANDER THE STREETS IN A DAZE FOR WEEKS, LOOKING FOR A NEW LOCATION... A FRESH START.

IT'S ALWAYS A TERRIBLE BLOW TO MY FAMILY.

AN EMPTY CASH REGISTER LEFT OPEN

AS IF TO SAY: DON'T BREAK IN HERE, IT'S NOT WORTH YOUR WHILE.

THERE'S NOTHING HERE OF VALUE.

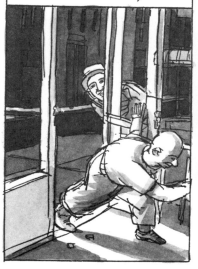
THESE FIXTURES AND DECORATIONS,

FROZEN HAMBURGERS AND CANNED POTATOES

ARE OF VALUE ONLY TO A MAN WITH THE KNOW-HOW

AND WILLINGNESS TO RUN A COFFEE SHOP.

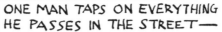
ONE MAN TAPS ON EVERYTHING HE PASSES IN THE STREET—

LIKE A STAGE MAGICIAN TRYING TO CONVINCE HIS AUDIENCE OF THE SOLIDITY OF HIS PROPS.

FOR A MOMENT, MR. KNIPL BELIEVES THAT THERE'S A FUTURE IN REAL ESTATE PHOTOGRAPHY,

...NOT ONLY THE LEGAL NECESSITY FOR PROPERTY OWNERS TO HAVE A PHOTOGRAPHIC RECORD OF THEIR HOLDINGS, BUT IN THE EVENT OF A SALE, THE PRESENCE OF A REAL ESTATE PHOTOGRAPHER IS ESSENTIAL...

FEELS SURE THAT WHAT HE JUST ATE WAS GENUINE TUNA FISH,

THAT THE BUILDING HOUSING HIS OFFICE IS STILL STANDING,

THAT THE COCHLEA OF HIS INNER EAR IS STILL FUNCTIONING

AND THAT THIS MAN HAS SIMPLY PASSED OUT OF EARSHOT.

JULIUS KNIPL
REAL ESTATE PHOTOGRAPHER

I FIRST MET MORRIS PULKOWITZ AS A YOUNG MAN, STARTING OUT IN THE HOSIERY BUSINESS

AS THOUGH THE SLICES CUT FROM A SINGLE SALAMI OVER MANY YEARS

HARD WORK AND DILIGENCE PAID OFF FOR THIS UNSCHOOLED IMMIGRANT. IN 1940, HE STARTED HIS OWN COMPANY

COULD SOMEHOW BE BROUGHT BACK TOGETHER IN THEIR ORIGINAL ORDER

FOR THE PAST FIFTY YEARS, WHENEVER YOU HEARD THE NAME 'PULKOWITZ,' YOU THOUGHT OF LADIES' HOSIERY.

AND WITH A SPECIFIC MEMORY OF HUNGER ASSOCIATED WITH EACH!

MORRIS AND HIS WIFE RAISED TWO BEAUTIFUL SONS AND A DAUGHTER

I LAST SAW MORRIS PULKOWITZ AT THE PHLEBITIS SOCIETY FUNDRAISER. HE WAS A GENEROUS MAN.

NO. FOR MR. KNIPL IT WAS MORE LIKE THE TASTE OF THE ONE SPICY INGREDIENT IN A PLATE OF SALAMI AND EGGS

THAT WOULD REPEAT ITSELF FOR YEARS TO COME.

67

IN ALL OF THE BUILDINGS SURROUNDING STRANGURY PARK, ONLY 35 MEN AND 4 WOMEN KNOW HOW TO PLAY PINOCHLE.

OF THESE, ONLY 3 MEN ACTUALLY PLAY THE GAME ON A REGULAR BASIS.

IN ALL OF THE DESK DRAWERS, IN ALL OF THESE BUILDINGS, NOT A SINGLE PINOCHLE DECK CAN BE FOUND.

THE KITCHEN OF THIS RESTAURANT WAS ONCE THE BACK ROOM OF THE GNADEN CAFÉ, WHERE THE GAME WAS PLAYED 24 HOURS A DAY.

ACCORDING TO THE 1938 EDITION OF HOYLE, NO RULES EXIST FOR GRACIOUSLY LEAVING A GAME TO EARN A LIVING, TO ATTEND RELIGIOUS SERVICES, OR TO ANSWER THE CALL OF NATURE.

IN THE NORTHWEST CORNER OF THE PARK STANDS A MONUMENT

IN MEMORY OF THOSE PINOCHLE PLAYERS LOST, BUT NOT NECESSARILY KILLED, DURING THE SECOND WORLD WAR.

WHEN A GARMENT COMES IN TO BE CLEANED, I'M CAREFUL TO EMPTY THE POCKETS

TICKET STUBS, BUS TRANSFERS, INVITATIONS, TOOTHPICKS... I DON'T THROW ANYTHING AWAY.

THANK YOU

WEEKS LATER, IN THE POCKET OF HIS LIGHTWEIGHT JACKET, MR. KNIPL FINDS THE STUB OF A TICKET FOR THE OBSERVATION DECK OF A FAMOUS SKYSCRAPER.

BUT CAN'T REMEMBER HAVING BEEN THERE,

IT'S THE WORK OF AN ECCENTRIC DRY CLEANER.

AFTER THE GARMENT'S NICE AND CLEAN, I TRY MY BEST TO PUT SOMETHING BACK INTO EVERY POCKET.

THOSE CLEAR MEMORIES OF LOW VISIBILITY,

OF FEELING A BUILDING SWAY IN THE WIND

AND OF A HOT DOG ON THE 104th FLOOR,

BELONG TO ANOTHER MAN.

SKEE-BALL FUN, ONE POINT?

69

RESTAURANT OWNERS HAVE COME TO ACCEPT

COULD I BORROW YOUR SALT?

THE INEVITABLE DISAPPEARANCE OF SALT AND PEPPER SHAKERS,

YOU GOT THE OIL AND VINEGAR OVER THERE?

THANKS

OIL AND VINEGAR BOTTLES,

I'M LOOKING FOR THE OIL AND VINEGAR.

KNIVES, FORKS

THANK YOU

AND SPOONS.

MY CUSTOMERS SWALLOW ALL THE TEASPOONS.

ALTHOUGH THESE ITEMS ARE NOW MANUFACTURED IN VAST QUANTITIES AND SOLD AT PRICES THAT MAKE THEIR LOSS NEGLIGIBLE TO AN INDIVIDUAL RESTAURATEUR,

I JUST HAD THE OIL AND VINEGAR HERE IN FRONT OF ME!

THEY STILL CAN NOT BE REPLACED AS QUICKLY AS THEY DISAPPEAR.

LOOK AROUND. LOOK AROUND.

Julius Knipl

WHILE U WAIT
ERATIONS

A SIGN IN THE WINDOW PROCLAIMS THE WILLINGNESS, OF AT LEAST THE STORE'S OWNER, TO HAVE HIS EMPLOYEES PERFORM A ROUTINE OF MANUAL LABOR UNDER CEASE-LESS PRESSURE AND ON A DAILY BASIS.

CUSTOMERS, COMPLETELY UNACQUAINTED WITH THE WORK INVOLVED, ARE ENCOURAGED TO LOOK ON FOR AMUSEMENT.

OVER THE YEARS, MOST OF THESE SIGNS HAVE FORTUNATELY BEEN REMOVED FROM STOREFRONT DISPLAYS.

ONLY IN THE SHOE REPAIR

AND KEY DUPLICATION BUSINESS DOES A VESTIGE OF THIS INHUMAN WORKING CONDITION STILL EXIST.

IN ONE CASE, THE CUSTOMER RENDERS HIMSELF INCAPABLE OF DOING ANYTHING BUT WAIT.

IN THE OTHER, DISTRUST COMPELS HIM TO WAIT.

THE SIGN HAS NOTHING TO DO WITH IT.

YOU WUNNA WAIT?

A FEEBLE MECHANICAL CLANG

FOLLOWED BY A BLAST OF STEAM FROM AN UPPER-STORY WINDOW

A SHOE TREE MANUFACTURER?

A YORTZHEIT CANDLE FACTORY?

A GOOD LUCK RING FOUNDRY?

A REBUILDER OF MALTED MIXERS?

AN ACCORDION STRAP FACTORY?

'JANK'

AN ELEVATOR-SHOE MAKER?

AND FOR A MOMENT, MR. KNIPL IS ASSURED THAT LIGHT MANUFACTURING STILL THRIVES IN THIS CITY.

AN INDOOR CLOTHESLINE MANUFACTURER?

FOR AS LONG AS MR. KNIPL CAN REMEMBER

A SMALL FLAME HAS ALWAYS BURNED

UNDER THIS OBLONG PAN OF STAINLESS STEEL.

A CERTAIN QUANTITY OF SAUERKRAUT IS THUS KEPT WARM

ALL DAY AND NIGHT.

THIS ETERNAL FLAME REMINDS HIM

A FRANK WITH MUSTARD AND SAUERKRAUT

OF THE NECESSITY FOR CHEAP FOOD.

50¢

50¢!?

JULIUS KNIPL
REAL ESTATE PHOTOGRAPHER

MR. KNIPL SOMETIMES GOES TO SIT IN THE PARK

JUST TO WATCH THE TRASH BEING SPEARED.

IN THE HANDS OF AN EXPERIENCED PARK ATTENDANT,

THERE EXISTS NO MORE PERFECT TOOL FOR LIFTING A SUCCESSION OF DISCARDED PAPERS FROM THE SOFT EARTH

THAN THIS SIMPLE WOODEN STICK WITH ITS LONG, PROTRUDING NAIL.

A FOOT DOCTOR'S FREE OFFER... THE FRONT PAGE OF A SOCIALIST NEWSPAPER...

FREE EXAMINATION
DR. LIONB...
UNITE
SECURITY PEACE

THE LID OF A COFFEE CONTAINER ... THE CELLOPHANE WRAPPER FROM A COUGH DROP...

I GUARANTEE YOU... IT'LL SMELL LIKE ROSES

FOR REASONS OF HYGIENE, ONE SALESMAN REFUSES TO PUT HIS EAR TO A PUBLIC PHONE.

EVEN IF YOU DON'T CLEAN EVERY DAY

HE HOLDS THE RECEIVER BARELY AN INCH AWAY

NO, NO, NO. THIS IS SOMETHING COMPLETELY NEW!

SO AS NOT TO INSULT ANY OF THE OTHER SALESMEN WHO USE THESE PAY PHONES AS THEIR OFFICE.

HOW MANY EMPLOYEES DO YOU HAVE? ...ALL MEN?

HE SELLS AIR FRESHEN-ING SYSTEMS DESIGNED FOR INSTITUTIONAL RESTROOMS.

YOU JUST HANG ONE UP IN EACH URINAL

A CASHEW SALESMAN HAPPENS TO SEE EVERYTHING

YOU HAVE TO SEE IT TO UNDERSTAND

AND THE NEXT DAY, AT LUNCH, EXPECTS MR. KNIPL TO SHARE HIS INDIGNATION.

I DON'T DENY THAT GERMS BREED INSIDE...

OF COURSE

BUT IF YOU OPERATE IN THE PUBLIC YOU HAVE TO TAKE YOUR CHANCES.

YOU'RE RIGHT

DO YOU THINK HE LIKES TO HANDLE DAMP MONEY FROM A SWEATY WALLET THAT'S BEEN IN MY BACK POCKET ALL DAY?

BY MEANS OF AN INGENIOUS ARRANGEMENT OF MIRRORS

A CASHIER IS ABLE TO SEE WHAT'S GOING ON IN A DISTANT AND OBSCURE CORNER OF THE STORE.

HE WATCHES SOMEONE CHOOSE A BRAND OF TOOTHPASTE.

HE SEES THE LABEL GRADUALLY COME LOOSE FROM A BOTTLE OF MOUTHWASH.

HE WATCHES A MAN ADJUST HIS UNDERWEAR.

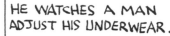

HE SEES A WOMAN QUICKLY EAT A SANDWICH BROUGHT FROM HOME

AND, FOR THE FIRST TIME, AFTER FIVE YEARS ON THE JOB, NOTICES THE COLOR OF THE FLOOR.

...A STYPTIC PENCIL? ...EXCUSE ME, I'M LOOKING FOR A STYPTIC PENCIL ...DO YOU CARRY STYPTIC PENCILS?

JULIUS KNIPL
REAL ESTATE
PHOTOGRAPHER

LATE EACH NIGHT, A MAN STEPS OUT OF HIS APARTMENT BUILDING

TO STAND IN THE STREET AND HAVE A GOOD COUGH.

IN THIS DEEP, RESONANT BOOM, MR. KNIPL CAN DISCERN

THE SOUND OF A STICKBALL BAT CONNECTING WITH A RUBBER BALL

THE SOUND OF BEER KEGS ROLLING IN THE STREET

A TIME-CLOCK STAMPING 5:08 P.M.

SOMEONE RIFFLING THROUGH THE PAGES OF A MEN'S MAGAZINE

THE OPENING OF A CAN OF CORNED BEEF HASH

AND THE SOUND OF THE POLICE TAKING AN APARTMENT DOOR OFF BY ITS HINGES.

77

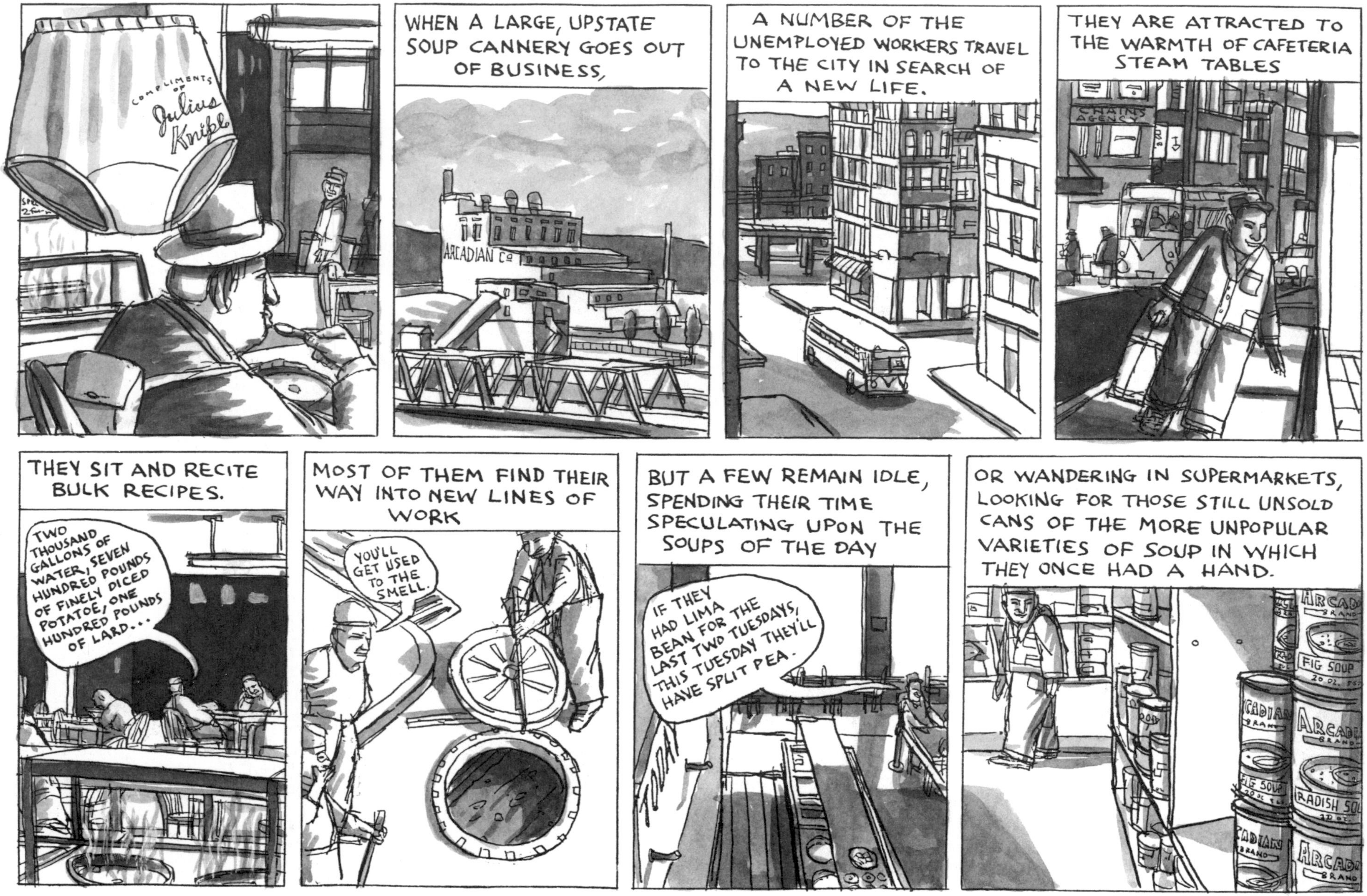
COMPLIMENTS OF Julius Knipl
WHEN A LARGE, UPSTATE SOUP CANNERY GOES OUT OF BUSINESS,
ARCADIAN Co
A NUMBER OF THE UNEMPLOYED WORKERS TRAVEL TO THE CITY IN SEARCH OF A NEW LIFE.
THEY ARE ATTRACTED TO THE WARMTH OF CAFETERIA STEAM TABLES
THEY SIT AND RECITE BULK RECIPES.
TWO THOUSAND GALLONS OF WATER, SEVEN HUNDRED POUNDS OF FINELY DICED POTATOE, ONE HUNDRED POUNDS OF LARD...
MOST OF THEM FIND THEIR WAY INTO NEW LINES OF WORK
YOU'LL GET USED TO THE SMELL.
BUT A FEW REMAIN IDLE, SPENDING THEIR TIME SPECULATING UPON THE SOUPS OF THE DAY
IF THEY HAD LIMA BEAN FOR THE LAST TWO TUESDAYS, THIS TUESDAY THEY'LL HAVE SPLIT PEA.
OR WANDERING IN SUPERMARKETS, LOOKING FOR THOSE STILL UNSOLD CANS OF THE MORE UNPOPULAR VARIETIES OF SOUP IN WHICH THEY ONCE HAD A HAND.
FIG SOUP

IN THE MIDDLE OF THE NIGHT, MR. KNIPL IS HALF AWAKENED BY A FRAGMENTARY RING OF HIS TELEPHONE.

Brrink.

AN OPEN SALAMI ON HIS KITCHEN TABLE BEGINS TO SWEAT.

TWO MEN, WHO OWE HIM MONEY, SIT IN AN ALL-NIGHT DELICATESSEN AND RENEW THEIR PLEDGE TO NEVER PAY.

A FORMERLY UNAPPEALING TOOTHPICK DISPENSER NOW BECKONS HIM.

for your pleasure
TAKE ONE

A TRUCK BACKS ONTO HIS MOTHER'S GRAVE.

KNIPL 1908-1971

HE REALIZES THAT HE'S GONE THROUGH A LIFETIME'S SUPPLY OF PAPER BAGS IN JUST FORTY YEARS

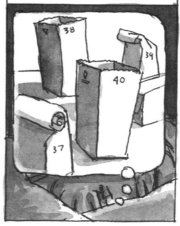

AND THEN EVERYTHING SMELLS OF POT ROAST.

THE PHONE COMPANY POSTPONES THE RANDOM TESTING OF TELEPHONE CONNECTIONS UNTIL LATE AT NIGHT SO AS NOT TO DISTURB THEIR CUSTOMERS.

AN UNOILED POSTCARD RACK

ACCENTUATES THE DISTANCE BETWEEN TWO POINTS OF INTEREST ON A SUNDAY AFTERNOON.

EVERYWHERE I LOOK— X-RAYS!

THESE POOR BLACK AND WHITE PHOTOGRAPHS

ONCE CIRCULATED EXCLUSIVELY AMONG TECHNICIANS AND MEDICAL DOCTORS.

YOU NEVER SAW SUCH A THING IN PUBLIC

FOR WHO TOOK NOTICE OF THOSE X-RAY LAB MESSENGERS WITH THEIR LEAD LINED CASES?

UNDERPAID MEN, TO WHOM A MISALIGNED SPINE OR SPOTTED LUNG WAS NO TRAGEDY.

A CHOCOLATE MALTED

TODAY, EVERYONE IS LEFT, WITH PROOF IN HAND, TO PLEAD THEIR OWN CASE

DURING A LUNCH BREAK OR AFTER WORK.

THERE'S NO RESEMBLANCE WHATSOEVER.

THE DAILY PIGEON

25¢

MR. KNIPL CAN'T STOP HIMSELF FROM READING

OBVIOUS LIES AND STATEMENTS OF THE MOST BANAL NATURE

WHEN THEY'RE SCREAMING FROM THE TOP OF A FRONT PAGE IN LARGE, BOLDFACE TYPE.

THE SMALL PRINT BELOW EXPLAINS NOTHING.

THESE STORIES CAN EXIST ONLY AS HEADLINES

PUBLISHED BY A MAN IN A **DIRTY** STALL NEXT DOOR TO THE RUECHAN THEATER

AND IN A PRINT RUN OF ONE.

ONE DELICATESSEN MAKES NO SECRET OF THE FACT

AH! HAROLD MERCURY.

HE WAS GOOD.

THAT ALMOST ALL OF ITS FAMOUS CUSTOMERS

REMEMBER ANNA KLIPS?

YOU DON'T GET SUCH TYPES ANYMORE.

ARE NOW DEAD.

FRANCIS CHEWINK

I HAVEN'T SEEN HIM IN ANYTHING LATELY

THEY FILL THE WALLS NICELY

REMEMBER KENT COULY?

I REMEMBER HIS OBITUARY.

AND CELEBRITIES TODAY ARE NOT AS FREE WITH SIGNED PHOTOGRAPHS AS THEY ONCE WERE.

THAT'S A NICE PICTURE OF ALFRED LASSO...

HE'S IN THE GRAVE TWENTY YEARS

SOME CUSTOMERS LOOK AROUND AND LOSE THEIR APPETITE

JUST A CUP OF NOODLE SOUP

OTHERS COUNT THEMSELVES LUCKY TO BE AMONG THE LIVING.

I'LL HAVE THE HAROLD MERCURY WITH A SIDE OF COLE-SLAW AND A CELERY TONIC... AND SOME MORE SOUR PICKLES PLEASE.

JULIUS KNIPL
REAL ESTATE PHOTOGRAPHER

ON THE BASIS OF CERTAIN STATISTICAL EVIDENCE, THE CITY TRANSIT AUTHORITY HAS ASSIGNED ONLY TWO BUSES TO THE #7 AURAPON AVENUE ROUTE.

IT IS A THREE AND A HALF MILE, GALOSH SHAPED ROUTE, WHICH PASSES BY

THE MAIN ENTRANCE TO THE CONVERTIBLE SOFA WORKERS' UNION CEMETERY,

A PICTURE FRAME SUPPLY YARD,

FRAME STOCK
24 HOUR
ACTIVE DRIVEWAY

THE MAIN OFFICE OF A NATIONAL DISTRIBUTOR OF COIN-OPERATED SCALES,

WEIGH YOUR FATE
SCALE CO.
CIGARS

THE PUBLIC SELTZER WORKS,

THE FAMOUS, BUT NOW EMPTY, 'BYZANTIUM SALT WATER POOL'

MUTTO
BYZANTIUM

AND THE 'M. OLGIN BALLROOM,' A COMMUNIST CATERING ESTABLISHMENT.

DISCOUNT
CHAIRS FURNITURE
OLGIN OLGIN

HOW LONG HAVE YOU BEEN WAITING?
BUS STOP

84

IN A RARE DISPLAY OF CIVIC INGENUITY,

THE DEPARTMENT OF HEALTH HAS ESTABLISHED A NUMBER OF PUBLIC MUSTARD FOUNTAINS IN THE MIDTOWN AREA

WHAT BETTER WAY OF IMPROVING A BLAND SECTION OF TOWN.

DURING THE LUNCH HOUR OF ANY BUSINESS DAY, THOUSANDS OF PEOPLE FIND THEMSELVES IN NEED OF THIS CONDIMENT

AND WHY SHOULD THEY BE ALLOWED TO FALL PREY TO A RAPACIOUS QUICK-LUNCH INDUSTRY?

SURELY, THE CITY, WITH ITS VAST RESOURCES, CAN PROVIDE EVERY CITIZEN IN NEED WITH A SHMIR OF MUSTARD—

A COMMON, BRIGHT YELLOW, DOMESTIC VARIETY—NOTHING FANCY—

JUST SOMETHING TO PIQUE THE JADED APPETITE OF AN OFFICE WORKER.

FOR SENTIMENTAL REASONS OF THEIR OWN, THE APARTMENT HOUSE DEVELOPERS OF THE EARLY 20th CENTURY WOULD BESTOW UPON EACH NEW BUILDING

THE NAME OF EITHER A SICKLY CHILD,

A RECENTLY DECEASED WIFE,

A FAVORITE VACATION SPOT

OR A MYTHOLOGICAL FIGURE.

UNDER A DOZEN COATS OF PAINT, CARELESSLY APPLIED OVER THE YEARS,

THESE NAMES HAD BECOME ALMOST INVISIBLE AND WERE, IN ALL CASES, SUPERSEDED

BY THOSE BRIGHT, NUMERIC DECALS

TO WHICH EACH TENANT IS NOW FREE TO ATTACH SOME PERSONAL SIGNIFICANCE.

QUICK! HURRY!

IN THE DAYS OF THE 'BIG EATERS'—

GIMME A BROMOL!

INDIVIDUALS WHO WOULD MATTER-OF-FACTLY HAVE EVERYTHING ON A RESTAURANT MENU—

THESE DISPENSERS HUNG EVERYWHERE.

AHH!

THE INVENTIONS OF CINEMASCOPE, INSTANT COFFEE AND THE BALLPOINT PEN ALL HAD THEIR GENESIS

HMM?

IN THOSE GLORIOUS MOMENTS OF MENTAL RELIEF FOLLOWING A BICARBONATE OF SODA.

A TINY PAPER CUP FULL OF POWDER AND A GLASS OF COOL WATER WERE BROUGHT WITH THE DESSERT

AND EACH CUSTOMER WOULD REPEAT TO HIMSELF...

DRINK IT WHILE IT FIZZES

ONE CREAM OF MUSHROOM

compliments of JULIUS KNIPL REAL ESTATE PHOTOGRAPHER

FROM EACH HANDFUL OF CHANGE HE COLLECTS,

A DOLLAR TWENTY-FIVE

THIS BUSINESSMAN REMOVES ALL OF THE PENNIES AND THROWS THEM INTO THE GARBAGE.

I CAN'T BE BOTHERED

HE BELIEVES THAT THESE SMALL, WORTHLESS OBJECTS OBSTRUCT THE COURSE OF HIS OTHERWISE HAPPY LIFE.

THEY ARE A RALLYING POINT FOR HIS ENEMIES,

HE HOLDS ONTO EACH ONE

AN OMEN OF COMMERCIAL FAILURE,

118, 119, 120, 121, 122 . . .

ACCOUNT FOR THE UNFAITHFULNESS OF HIS WIFE,

AND, IN TIME, BRING ABOUT A FATAL DISEASE.

THE SMALLER THE DENOMINATION, THE MORE GERMS IT CARRIES!

AH, A PENNY! IT'S MY LUCKY DAY.

A MAN STANDS IN THE STREET, OBLIVIOUS TO HIS PHYSICAL SURROUNDINGS.

7:30 P.M., 'THE MINERAL OIL HOUR'

HE DREAMS OF A CITY OF PLYWOOD SKYSCRAPERS,

8:30, 'THE WINDOW WASHER,' DRAMA

OF GOOD-NATURED MEN IN TUXEDOS,

9:00 P.M., 'YOUR SECRET ADMIRER,' COMEDY

OF WOMEN WITH BOUNDLESS ENERGY

9:30 P.M., 'SOL BOURÉE DANCE CLUB'

AND OF HIGHLY TRAINED ANIMALS.

10:00 P.M., 'HYDE BROS. VARIETY SHOW'

WHEN IT GETS TOO DARK TO READ,

HE GOES INTO THE NEAREST CAFETERIA.

IT'S 9:15 P.M. 'YOUR SECRET ADMIRER' IS ON RIGHT NOW!

THROUGH THE USE OF CHEAP, READY-MADE SIGNS

EMPLOYEES MUST WASH THEIR HANDS. *Sect. 84 Health Dept.*

AND HASTILY HAND-LETTERED NOTICES,

WASH HAND AFTER USING TOILET

THE TRUE INTENT OF AN IMPORTANT HEALTH DEPARTMENT STATUTE HAS BECOME HOPELESSLY OBSCURED,

MEN

THE ACTUAL WORDING SIMPLIFIED AND ABRIDGED BEYOND RECOGNITION.

NO HOT WATER

WASH YOUR HANDS

AS COMPOSED BY A COMMITTEE OF SANITATION ENGINEERS IN 1921,

...THE TRUST EXTENDED TO ONE INDIVIDUAL TO ANOTHER MUST NOT STOP AT THE LAVATORY DOOR. IT IS IN THESE PRIVATE MOMENTS THAT ONE MUST REAFFIRM THE TACIT AGREEMENT THAT EXISTS BETWEEN ALL MEN AND WOMEN, REGARDLESS OF HYGIENIC CONSIDERATIONS, REGARDLESS OF WHETHER ONE'S HANDS ARE SOILED OR NOT...

SECTION 84 OF THE PUBLIC HEALTH CODE WAS AN ATTEMPT TO SET FORTH, BY MEANS OF A DELICATELY WROUGHT CHAIN OF ARGUMENTATION, A LEGAL BASIS FOR HUMAN DECENCY —

WASH HANDS

NO SOAP ...NO PAPER TOWELS

ALL OF WHICH IS NOW LOST IN THE FLUORESCENT GLARE OF A RESTAURANT TOILET.

MEN

PUSH

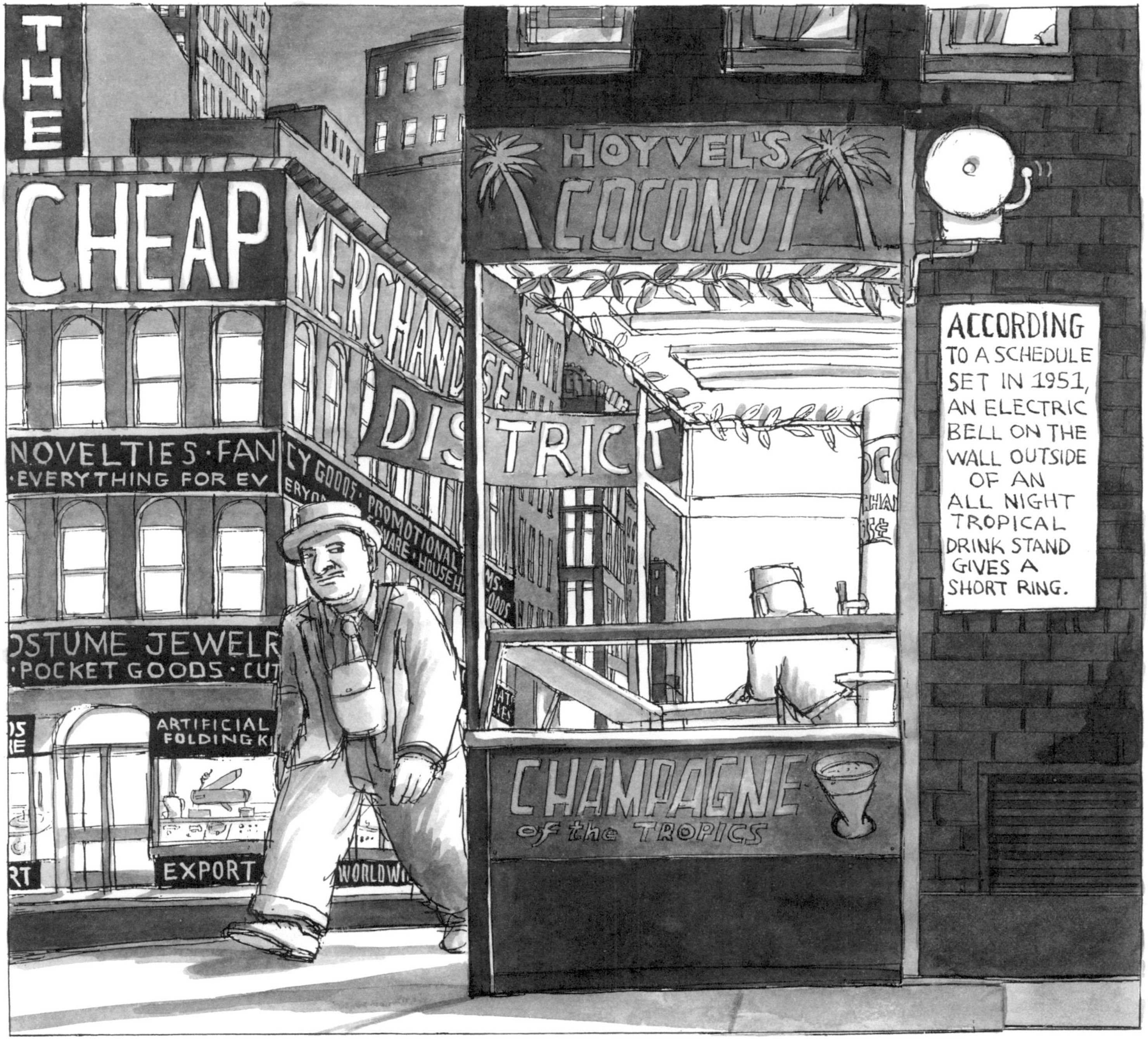
THE
CHEAP MERCHANDISE DISTRICT
NOVELTIES · FANCY GOODS
· EVERYTHING FOR EV
PROMOTIONAL
OSTUME JEWELR
· POCKET GOODS · CUT
ARTIFICIAL
FOLDING K
EXPORT
WORLDWI
HOYVEL'S COCONUT
CHAMPAGNE of the TROPICS
ACCORDING TO A SCHEDULE SET IN 1951, AN ELECTRIC BELL ON THE WALL OUTSIDE OF AN ALL NIGHT TROPICAL DRINK STAND GIVES A SHORT RING.

LIKE THE BELL SIGNALING THE START OF AN AMUSEMENT-PARK RIDE

OR SOME OTHER HOPEFUL AND ENERGETIC ROUTINE.

A LARGE COCONUT CHAMPAGNE

IN THE OPINION OF CERTAIN CONCESSIONAIRES, THE RINGING OF A BELL OR BANGING ON A GRILL WITH A SPATULA AT IRREGULAR INTERVALS OF TIME, IS A SURE METHOD OF INCREASING SALES.

THE SOUND STIMULATES PEDESTRIANS INTO MOTION

EITHER TOWARD THE STAND TO BUY A DRINK, OR AWAY, ONCE THEY'VE HAD IT.

THE WHOLE DAY SHOT...!

AND AT THIS HOUR, WINDOW SHOPPERS STILL LINGER BEFORE THE CHEAP MERCHANDISE HOUSES.

HE SAW MY NAME ON A BALLPOINT PEN

I SAW YOUR NAME ON A BALL-POINT PEN

ACROSS THE STREET, SOMEONE'S GIVEN UP ON A CONTAINER OF 'GOOD BOY ORANGE DRINK.'

THEN HE ASKS ME IF I KNOW ROSSELL AVENUE

THE NIGHT AIR IS SUDDENLY SWEETENED BY THE FRAGRANCE OF COMMERCIAL BAKING.

IF I KNOW ROSSELL AVENUE

THAT MORNING, MR. KNIPL WALKED THE LENGTH OF ROSSELL AVENUE.

WEDDING CAKE DECORATION SHOWROOMS

PAWN SHOPS

STORE-FRONT CHURCHES

USED TIRE STORES

ROOMING HOUSES

SECOND-STORY RESTAURANTS

BUSY FUNERAL PARLORS

READY-MADE WIG SALONS

BOILER YARDS

DAY-OLD BREAD STORES

HERE, NUMBER 801

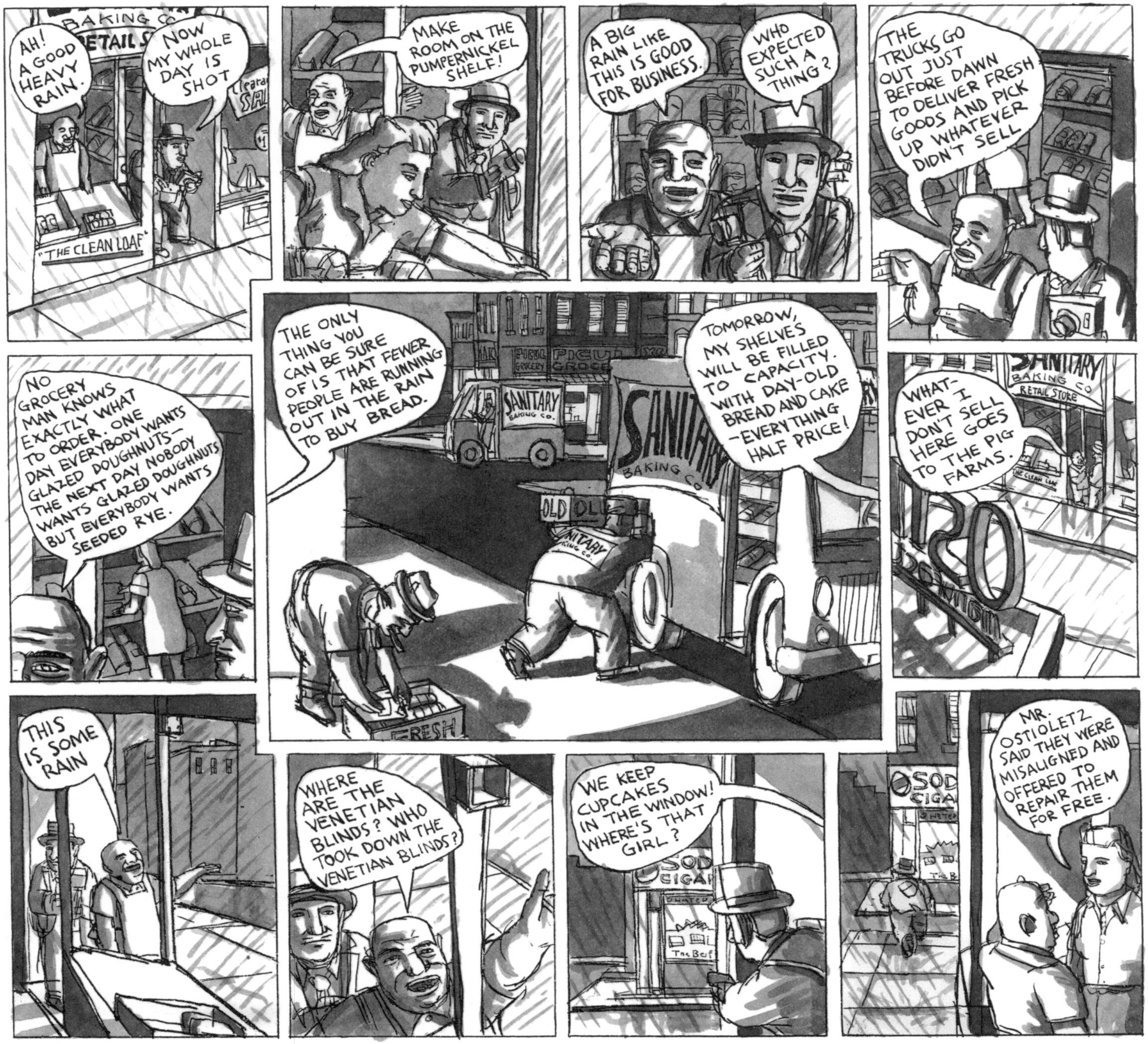
BAKING CO
RETAIL S
AH! A GOOD HEAVY RAIN.
NOW MY WHOLE DAY IS SHOT
"THE CLEAN LOAF"
MAKE ROOM ON THE PUMPERNICKEL SHELF!
A BIG RAIN LIKE THIS IS GOOD FOR BUSINESS.
WHO EXPECTED SUCH A THING?
THE TRUCKS GO OUT JUST BEFORE DAWN TO DELIVER FRESH GOODS AND PICK UP WHATEVER DIDN'T SELL
NO GROCERY MAN KNOWS EXACTLY WHAT TO ORDER. ONE DAY EVERYBODY WANTS GLAZED DOUGHNUTS— THE NEXT DAY NOBODY WANTS GLAZED DOUGHNUTS BUT EVERYBODY WANTS SEEDED RYE.
THE ONLY THING YOU CAN BE SURE OF IS THAT FEWER PEOPLE ARE RUNNING OUT IN THE RAIN TO BUY BREAD.
SANITARY BAKING CO.
TOMORROW, MY SHELVES WILL BE FILLED TO CAPACITY. WITH DAY-OLD BREAD AND CAKE —EVERYTHING HALF PRICE!
FRESH
SANITARY BAKING CO RETAIL STORE
WHAT-EVER I DON'T SELL HERE GOES TO THE PIG FARMS.
THIS IS SOME RAIN
WHERE ARE THE VENETIAN BLINDS? WHO TOOK DOWN THE VENETIAN BLINDS?
WE KEEP CUPCAKES IN THE WINDOW! WHERE'S THAT GIRL?
MR. OSTIOLETZ SAID THEY WERE MISALIGNED AND OFFERED TO REPAIR THEM FOR FREE.

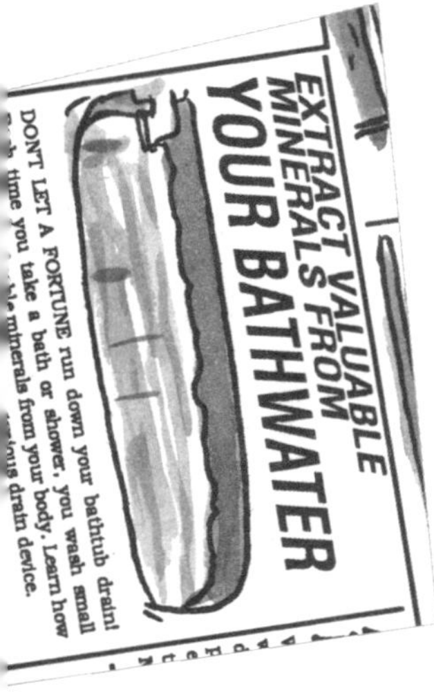
EXTRACT VALUABLE MINERALS FROM
YOUR BATHWATER
DONT LET A FORTUNE run down your bathtub drain!
time you take a bath or shower, you wash small
minerals from your body. Learn how
drain device.

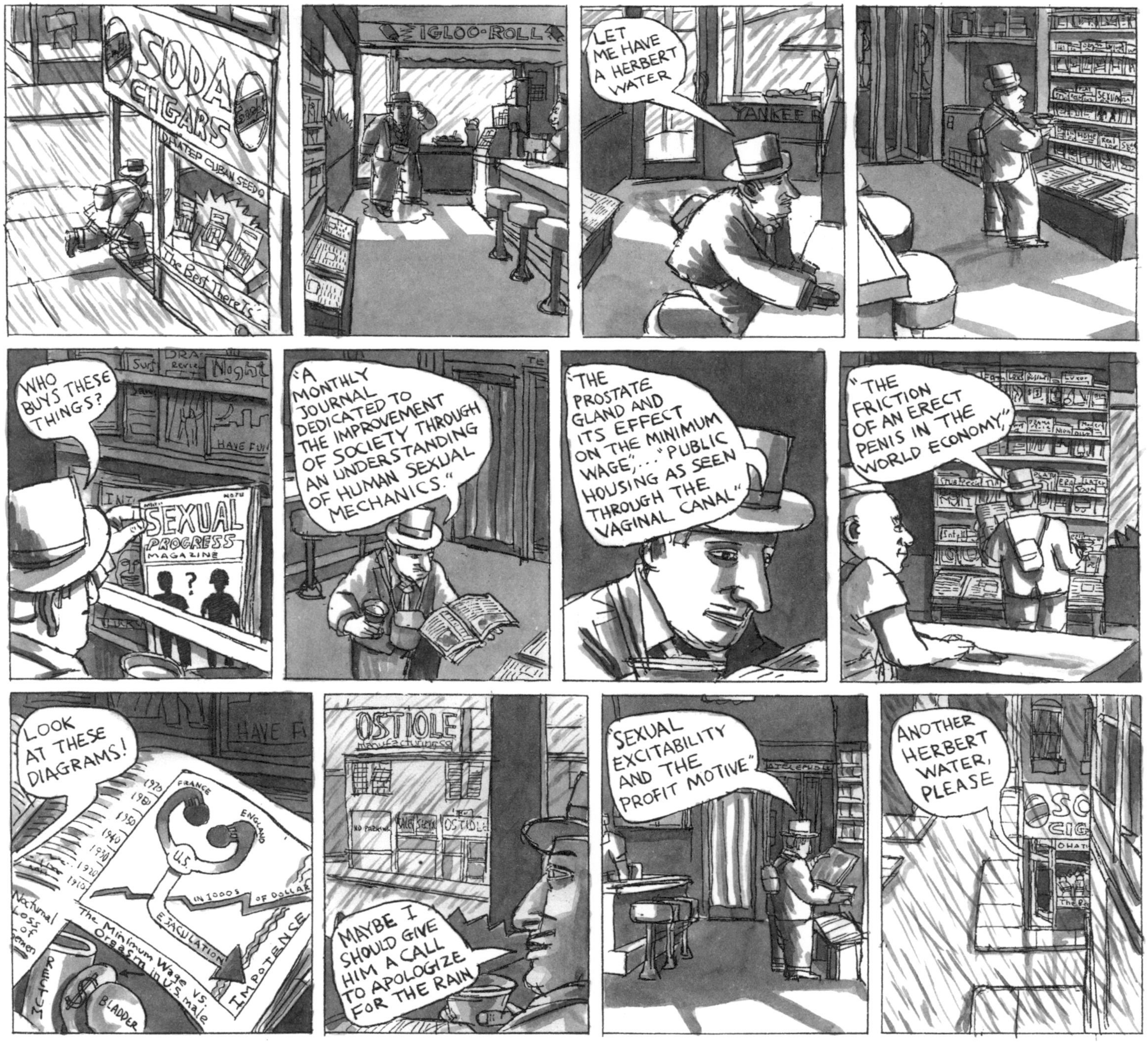
SODA
CIGARS
The Best There Is
IGLOO-ROLL
LET ME HAVE A HERBERT WATER
YANKEE
WHO BUYS THESE THINGS?
SEXUAL PROGRESS MAGAZINE
"A MONTHLY JOURNAL DEDICATED TO THE IMPROVEMENT OF SOCIETY THROUGH AN UNDERSTANDING OF HUMAN SEXUAL MECHANICS."
"THE PROSTATE GLAND AND ITS EFFECT ON THE MINIMUM WAGE";..."PUBLIC HOUSING AS SEEN THROUGH THE VAGINAL CANAL"
"THE FRICTION OF AN ERECT PENIS IN THE WORLD ECONOMY"
LOOK AT THESE DIAGRAMS!
FRANCE
ENGLAND
U.S.
IN 1000S OF DOLLARS
EJACULATION
IMPOTENCE
The Minimum Wage vs. Orgasm in U.S. male
Nocturnal Loss of Semen
BLADDER
OSTIOLE
MAYBE I SHOULD GIVE HIM A CALL TO APOLOGIZE FOR THE RAIN
"SEXUAL EXCITABILITY AND THE PROFIT MOTIVE"
ANOTHER HERBERT WATER, PLEASE

ACROSS THE STREET, IN A SECOND FLOOR, PRIVATE OFFICE.

MARLON OSTIOLETZ LOOKS THROUGH HIS MAIL.

MY FATHER'S DEAD EIGHT MONTHS, BUT THEY KEEP SENDING IT.

MOST OF THEIR SUBSCRIBERS ARE DEAD BY NOW, BUT THEY WON'T GIVE UP AS LONG AS THEY HAVE THE MONEY TO PUBLISH.

THEY HAD SOME BIG CONTRIBUTORS. MY FATHER GAVE THOUSANDS OVER THE YEARS.

HE READ, OR AT LEAST BOUGHT, EVERYTHING ON THE SUBJECT. SEXUAL HYGIENE PAMPHLETS, PRIVATELY PRINTED SEXOLOGY BOOKS, UROLOGY MANUALS FOR LAYMEN—IT WAS HIS WAY OF MAKING SENSE OF WHAT HE SAW IN THE NEWSPAPERS.

THIS CONGRESSMAN HAS A HYPERACTIVE PITUITARY GLAND.

AND THEN, WHEN HE DIED, THOSE FRIENDS OF HIS...

MARASMUS FUNERAL HOME

521

ALFRED SMOLTZ, SARDINE IMPORTER

JACK LOURAY, THE TRAFFIC LIGHT MANUFACTURER

SIDNEY WASSERMAN, THE 'GOOD BOY' ORANGE DRINK BOTTLER

YOUR FATHER WAS A GREAT FRIEND OF THE MAGAZINE AND SO WE WERE WONDERING...

HAD THE NERVE TO ASK, AT THE FUNERAL, IF HE LEFT ANYTHING TO THE MAGAZINE!

ON THURSDAY NIGHTS, HE'D GO STRAIGHT FROM THIS OFFICE TO THE GARDEN OF EDEN CAFETERIA.

HE DRAGGED ME ALONG A COUPLE OF TIMES WHEN I WAS A KID — THEY NEEDED YOUNG BLOOD. HUNDREDS OF MIDDLE-AGED MEN WOULD EAT A QUICK MEAL AND THEN TIE UP EVERY TABLE IN THE PLACE WITH A COFFEE OR A BAKED APPLE, TALKING, ARGUING, EXCHANGING PAMPHLETS, TRYING TO ILLUMINATE THE DARKEST CORNERS OF HUMAN BEHAVIOR UNTIL TWO OR THREE O'CLOCK IN THE MORNING.

MY FATHER HAD SOMETHING TO SAY TO EVERYBODY.

NUPERCAINAL OINTMENT! THAT'S WHAT THIS CITY NEEDS

HE POINTED ACROSS THE STREET TO THE BRILLIANTLY LIT OFFICES OF 'SEXUAL PROGRESS MAGAZINE'

THEY DON'T GO HOME AT 5 O'CLOCK!

YOU'LL FIND THE ROOT OF CAPITALISM AT THE BASE OF THE URETHRA!

WHEN THE RICH FORNICATE, THE POOR SWEAT!

YOU'RE NOT TOO YOUNG TO UNDERSTAND THESE THINGS

THE INDUSTRIAL REVOLUTION IS STILL GOING ON IN OUR UNDERPANTS

AN ENTIRE ECONOMY BASED ON MENSTRUAL CYCLES . . .

IN FRONT OF ME, THEY OPENLY DISCUSSED VAGINAL MEMBRANES, SCROTAL ANATOMY AND THE COMPOSITION OF SEMEN,

THE FIVE RICHEST MEN IN THIS COUNTRY ALL HAVE PROSTATE TROUBLE

HOW ELSE COULD ONE EXPLAIN THE POVERTY, INJUSTICE AND CRUELTY THAT EXISTED ON THE OTHER SIDE OF THE PLATE GLASS WINDOW?

AT ELEVEN O'CLOCK, THE EDITOR OF 'SEXUAL PROGRESS MAGAZINE,' MOISHE NUSTRIL, CAME IN FOR PIE AND COFFEE.

EVERYBODY LISTENED WHEN HE SPOKE.

OUR DAYS ARE RULED BY OUR NIGHTS

IT WAS ALL THEORETICAL KNOWLEDGE. THESE WERE MARRIED MEN WHO DIDN'T RUN AROUND.

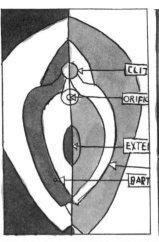

LIKE THE SMALL LANDLORD WHO'S A PROFESSED COMMUNIST OR THE ANARCHIST WITH A JOB IN THE POST OFFICE —FOR THESE MEN, TALK WAS ENOUGH.

THE ONLY VAGINAL MEMBRANES MY FATHER KNEW WERE DIAGRAMATIC ONES IN SMALL CIRCULATION MAGAZINES

CLIT
ORIFIC
EXTE
BART

SANITARY
BAKING CO
RETAIL STORE

MEANWHILE, HE LET THE BUSINESS RUN ITSELF INTO THE GROUND.

VENETIAN BLINDS BECAME AN INVISIBLE COMMODITY. HANGING EVERYWHERE BUT SEEN BY NO ONE.

CHECK OUT TIME: 8AM

OLD LUST

PLEASE DO NOT URINATE IN THE SINK

HOTEL

JOHNSON KEY-CHAIN COMPANY

ALL THIS HAS TO CHANGE!

FIRST, I NEED UP-TO-DATE PHOTOS OF THE FACTORY —SOMETHING TO SHOW INVESTORS AND OTHER INTERESTED PARTIES

I ALREADY HAVE A REAL ESTATE PHOTOGRAPHER ON THE JOB.

JULIU
REAL ES
KNIPL
PHOTOGRAPHER

SOD
CIGAR
"The Best Thin

HE SAW MY NAME ON A BALLPOINT PEN.

SEEL
TRY
ONE
SPECIAL

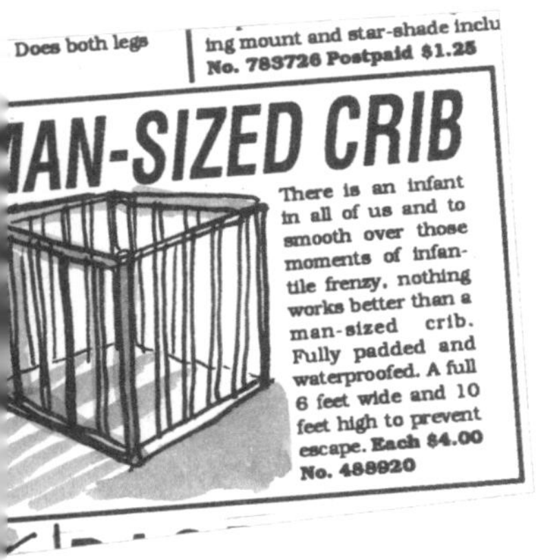
Does both legs
ing mount and star-shade inclu
No. 783726 Postpaid $1.25
AN-SIZED CRIB
There is an infant in all of us and to smooth over those moments of infantile frenzy, nothing works better than a man-sized crib. Fully padded and waterproofed. A full 6 feet wide and 10 feet high to prevent escape. Each $4.00
No. 488920

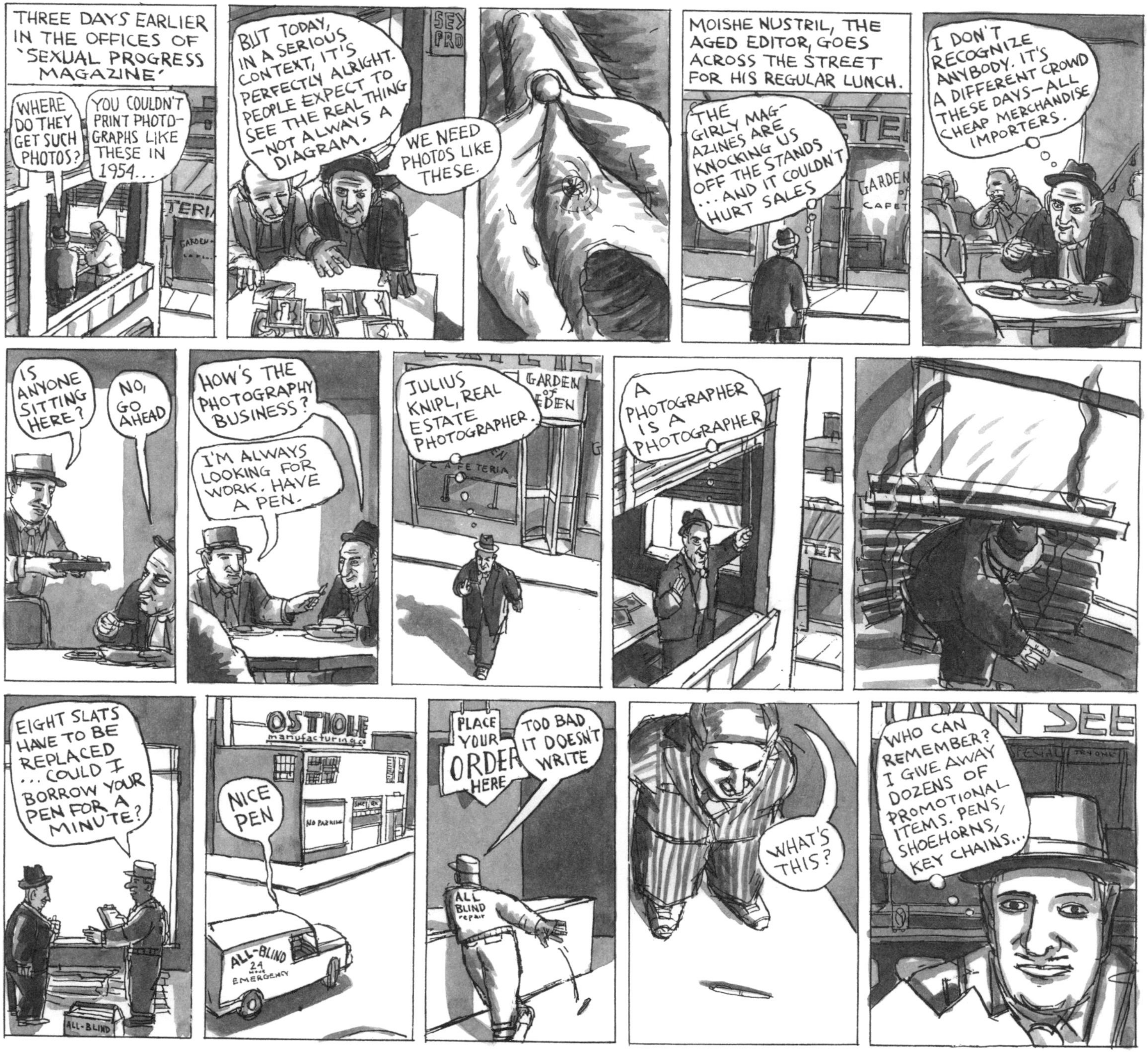
THREE DAYS EARLIER IN THE OFFICES OF 'SEXUAL PROGRESS MAGAZINE'
WHERE DO THEY GET SUCH PHOTOS?
YOU COULDN'T PRINT PHOTOGRAPHS LIKE THESE IN 1954...
BUT TODAY, IN A SERIOUS CONTEXT, IT'S PERFECTLY ALRIGHT. PEOPLE EXPECT TO SEE THE REAL THING —NOT ALWAYS A DIAGRAM.
WE NEED PHOTOS LIKE THESE.
MOISHE NUSTRIL, THE AGED EDITOR, GOES ACROSS THE STREET FOR HIS REGULAR LUNCH.
THE GIRLY MAGAZINES ARE KNOCKING US OFF THE STANDS ...AND IT COULDN'T HURT SALES
I DON'T RECOGNIZE ANYBODY. IT'S A DIFFERENT CROWD THESE DAYS—ALL CHEAP MERCHANDISE IMPORTERS.
IS ANYONE SITTING HERE?
NO, GO AHEAD
HOW'S THE PHOTOGRAPHY BUSINESS?
I'M ALWAYS LOOKING FOR WORK. HAVE A PEN.
JULIUS KNIPL, REAL ESTATE PHOTOGRAPHER.
GARDEN of EDEN
CAFETERIA
A PHOTOGRAPHER IS A PHOTOGRAPHER
EIGHT SLATS HAVE TO BE REPLACED ...COULD I BORROW YOUR PEN FOR A MINUTE?
ALL-BLIND
OSTIOLE
manufacturing co
NO PARKING
NICE PEN
ALL-BLIND
24 HOUR
EMERGENCY
PLACE YOUR ORDER HERE
TOO BAD IT DOESN'T WRITE
ALL BLIND repair
WHAT'S THIS?
WHO CAN REMEMBER? I GIVE AWAY DOZENS OF PROMOTIONAL ITEMS. PENS, SHOEHORNS, KEY CHAINS...

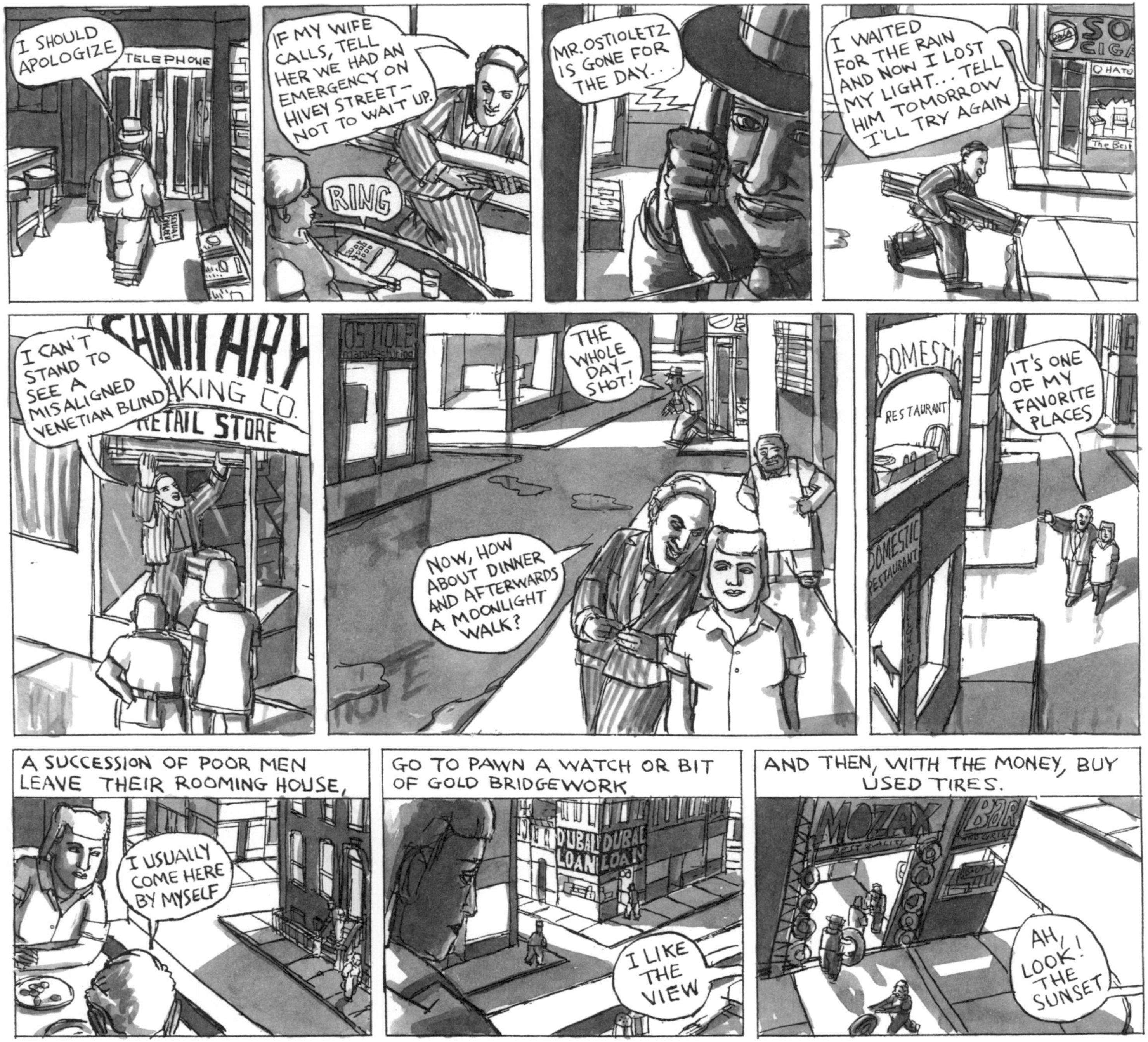
I SHOULD APOLOGIZE
TELEPHONE
IF MY WIFE CALLS, TELL HER WE HAD AN EMERGENCY ON HIVEY STREET— NOT TO WAIT UP.
RING
MR. OSTIOLETZ IS GONE FOR THE DAY...
I WAITED FOR THE RAIN AND NOW I LOST MY LIGHT... TELL HIM TOMORROW I'LL TRY AGAIN
I CAN'T STAND TO SEE A MISALIGNED VENETIAN BLIND
SANITARY
KING CO.
RETAIL STORE
THE WHOLE DAY-SHOT!
NOW, HOW ABOUT DINNER AND AFTERWARDS A MOONLIGHT WALK?
DOMESTIC
RESTAURANT
IT'S ONE OF MY FAVORITE PLACES
A SUCCESSION OF POOR MEN LEAVE THEIR ROOMING HOUSE,
I USUALLY COME HERE BY MYSELF
GO TO PAWN A WATCH OR BIT OF GOLD BRIDGEWORK
DUBAL LOAN
I LIKE THE VIEW
AND THEN, WITH THE MONEY, BUY USED TIRES.
MOZAX
BAR
AH, LOOK! THE SUNSET

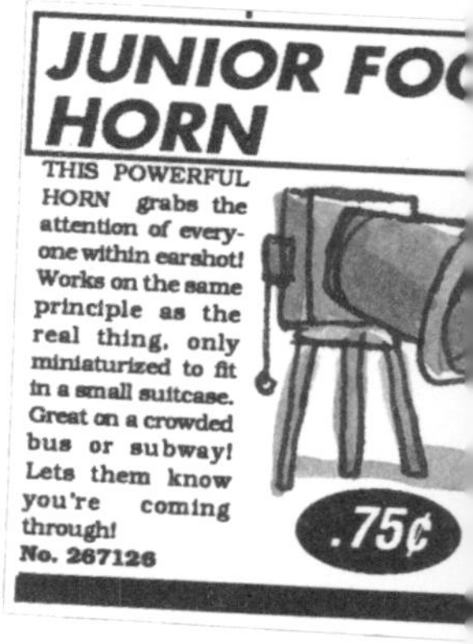
JUNIOR FO
HORN
THIS POWERFUL HORN grabs the attention of everyone within earshot! Works on the same principle as the real thing, only miniaturized to fit in a small suitcase. Great on a crowded bus or subway! Lets them know you're coming through!
No. 267126
.75¢

THOSE COMPANIES DEVOTED TO THE SELLING OF LOW-PRICED, POORLY-MADE GOODS OF ALL DESCRIPTION HAVE, SINCE THE LATE 1950s, CHOSEN TO DO BUSINESS IN THIS SECTION OF TOWN.

ALTHOUGH DISPARAGED BY THE GENERAL PUBLIC AND HELD IN LOW ESTEEM BY OTHER BUSINESSMEN, THE CHEAP MERCHANDISE DISTRICT IS, IN FACT, THE TRUE COMMERCIAL CORE OF THIS CITY.

AS ONE TRAVELS AWAY FROM HERE, ALONG ROSSELL AVENUE, THE CITY'S ENTREPRENEURIAL ENERGY SEEMS TO VISIBLY PETER OUT —

DULL STOREFRONTS MATTER-OF-FACTLY CATER TO MAN'S MOST BASIC NEEDS.

IN THE OTHER DIRECTION LIES ROMAN BOULEVARD, WITH ITS ART GALLERIES AND CORSET SALONS.

HERE, THE RAREFIED TASTES OF THE RICH ARE SATISFIED IN THE MOST IMAGINATIVE WAYS POSSIBLE.

IT IS, HOWEVER, TO THE CHEAP MERCHANDISE DISTRICT THAT EVERYONE MUST, AT SOME TIME OR ANOTHER IN THEIR CONSUMER LIFE, COME TO SHOP.

EACH 'HOUSE' BOASTS OF THE VAST NUMBER OF ITEMS IN STOCK—ALL DESCRIBED IN THICK, SEASONAL CATALOGS AND DISPLAYED IN BRILLIANTLY LIT WINDOWS.

THE MERCHANDISE RANGES OVER A COMPLETE SPECTRUM OF UTILITY—FROM A 10-IN-1 POCKET TOOL TO A CIGARETTE SMOKING BISQUE MONKEY.

THIS IS THE SOURCE OF THAT MERCHANDISE FOUND HANGING ON CARDS IN THE BACK OF CANDY STORES,

OR BETWEEN GLASS DIVIDERS ON THE COUNTERS OF FIVE-AND-TEN-CENT STORES

OR IN THE PRIZE SHOWCASE ADJOINING A SKEE-BALL ALLEY,

OR HANDED OUT, FREE OF CHARGE, AFTER BEING IMPRINTED WITH THE NAME OF SOME BUSINESS.

IN THE DESIGN AND MANUFACTURE OF EVERYTHING, THERE IS A BLATANT LACK OF WORTH.

IT IS THE DEFECTIVE MORTAR THAT MANAGES TO HOLD EACH CONSUMER ENTHRALLED FOR THE BRIEF SPAN OF A LIFETIME.

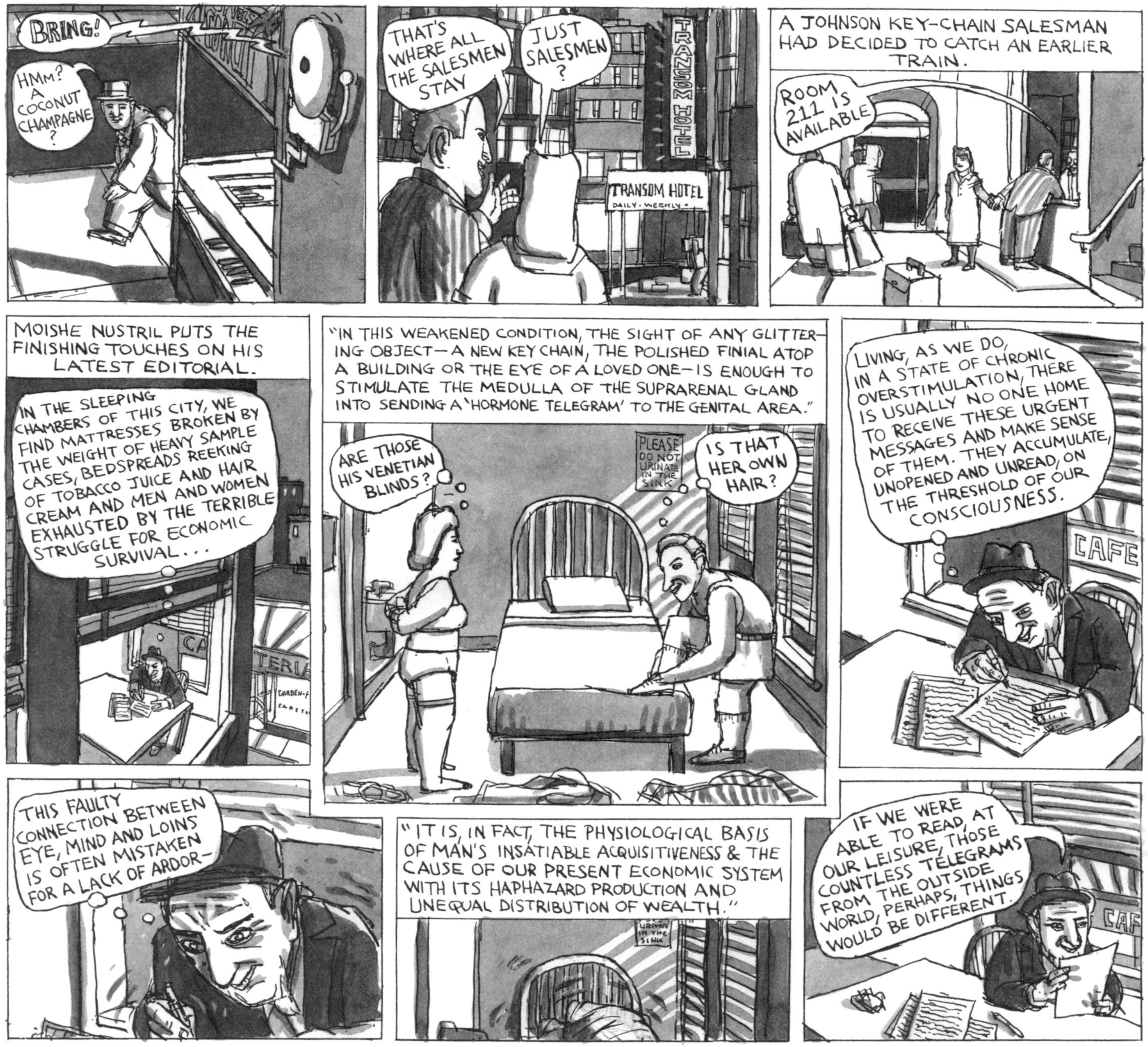
BRING!
HMM? A COCONUT CHAMPAGNE?
THAT'S WHERE ALL THE SALESMEN STAY
JUST SALESMEN?
TRANSOM HOTEL
TRANSOM HOTEL
DAILY - WEEKLY
A JOHNSON KEY-CHAIN SALESMAN HAD DECIDED TO CATCH AN EARLIER TRAIN.
ROOM 211 IS AVAILABLE
MOISHE NUSTRIL PUTS THE FINISHING TOUCHES ON HIS LATEST EDITORIAL.
IN THE SLEEPING CHAMBERS OF THIS CITY, WE FIND MATTRESSES BROKEN BY THE WEIGHT OF HEAVY SAMPLE CASES, BEDSPREADS REEKING OF TOBACCO JUICE AND HAIR CREAM AND MEN AND WOMEN EXHAUSTED BY THE TERRIBLE STRUGGLE FOR ECONOMIC SURVIVAL...
"IN THIS WEAKENED CONDITION, THE SIGHT OF ANY GLITTERING OBJECT—A NEW KEY CHAIN, THE POLISHED FINIAL ATOP A BUILDING OR THE EYE OF A LOVED ONE—IS ENOUGH TO STIMULATE THE MEDULLA OF THE SUPRARENAL GLAND INTO SENDING A 'HORMONE TELEGRAM' TO THE GENITAL AREA."
ARE THOSE HIS VENETIAN BLINDS?
PLEASE DO NOT URINATE IN THE SINK
IS THAT HER OWN HAIR?
LIVING, AS WE DO, IN A STATE OF CHRONIC OVERSTIMULATION, THERE IS USUALLY NO ONE HOME TO RECEIVE THESE URGENT MESSAGES AND MAKE SENSE OF THEM. THEY ACCUMULATE, UNOPENED AND UNREAD, ON THE THRESHOLD OF OUR CONSCIOUSNESS.
CAFE
THIS FAULTY CONNECTION BETWEEN EYE, MIND AND LOINS IS OFTEN MISTAKEN FOR A LACK OF ARDOR—
"IT IS, IN FACT, THE PHYSIOLOGICAL BASIS OF MAN'S INSATIABLE ACQUISITIVENESS & THE CAUSE OF OUR PRESENT ECONOMIC SYSTEM WITH ITS HAPHAZARD PRODUCTION AND UNEQUAL DISTRIBUTION OF WEALTH."
IF WE WERE ABLE TO READ, AT OUR LEISURE, THOSE COUNTLESS TELEGRAMS FROM THE OUTSIDE WORLD, PERHAPS, THINGS WOULD BE DIFFERENT.
CAF

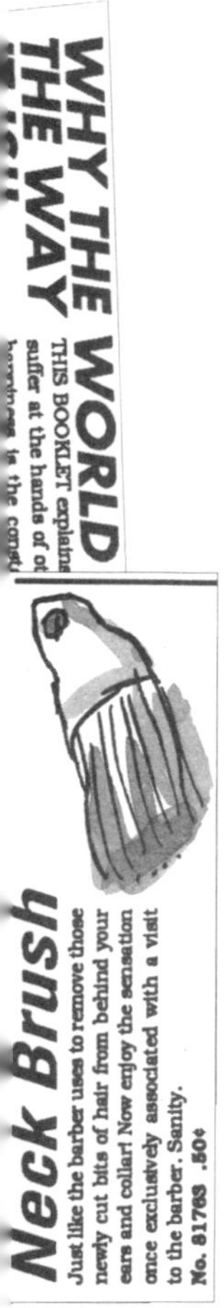
WHY THE WORLD
THE WAY
THIS BOOKLET explains
suffer at the hands of ot
Neck Brush
Just like the barber uses to remove those newly cut bits of hair from behind your ears and collar! Now enjoy the sensation once exclusively associated with a visit to the barber. Sanity.
No. 81763 .50¢

WITHIN THE CHEAP MERCHANDISE DISTRICT ARE A FEW NARROW, LOW-RENT OFFICE BUILDINGS OCCUPIED BY CLIPPING BUREAUS, STENOTYPE AGENCIES, FAILED LAWYERS AND OTHER MARGINAL BUSINESSES.

106

EVEN AT THIS HOUR, SALESMEN WAIT IN DOORWAYS.

THE GARDEN OF EATING. THEY'RE OPEN ALL NIGHT.

LOOKING OUT FOR AN EXTRA COMMISSION.

YOU'RE UNDER NO OBLIGATION TO STOP... I HAPPEN TO BE GOING IN YOUR DIRECTION.

AND WANTED TO LET YOU KNOW ABOUT A NEW ITEM ...

YOU'LL NEVER BE CAUGHT BY SURPRISE AGAIN...

SOMETHING NEW!
HAT BAND RAIN FORECASTER

FAIR TURNS BLUE ↔ RAIN TURNS PINK

10¢ EACH

You'll never be caught by surprise again when you wear this hat band rain forecaster! Years of experience have proven that the utmost reliance can be placed upon the simple yet scientific principles involved. When rain is imminent and the atmosphere becomes moist the band turns pink. When fine weather is expected → blue. Lilac indicates unsettled weather. No. 97... $2.00 per dozen

EACH IMPRINTED WITH YOUR COMPANY'S NAME AT NO EXTRA COST.

A DOZEN FOR NOW ... THE NAME IS JULIUS KNIPL...

WHERE WAS THAT SHOWCASE WITH THOSE BEAUTIFUL KEY CHAINS?

SUDDENLY, THE NARROW STREETS ARE FULL OF TRAILER TRUCKS MAKING THEIR MORNING DELIVERIES OF NEW MERCHANDISE.

CURB PAINTERS

CAFETERIA

GARDEN of EDEN

SO THIS IS WHEN IT'S DONE.

WE HAVE TO WORK THESE HOURS SO AS NOT TO ALARM THE GENERAL PUBLIC.

THEY'LL FIND OUT SOON ENOUGH WHAT HAPPENS WHEN YOU MOVE A BUS STOP. YOU SEE, IT'S ALL LINKED UP WITH PEDESTRIAN FOOTPATHS AND BIG BUSINESS.

A CHANGE LIKE THIS WILL KILL THE CAFETERIA. I GIVE IT TEN YEARS AT MOST. THAT'S ALL.

THAT'S ALL?

THE NEXT TIME YOU WANT SOMETHING TO EAT, THIS PLACE WILL BE GONE!

AND THIS WHOLE CHEAP MERCHANDISE DISTRICT IS ON THE WAY OUT. THIRTY, FORTY YEARS FROM NOW OUR GRANDCHILDREN WON'T KNOW IT EVER EXISTED!

THAT IS, IF WE EVER HAVE GRANDCHILDREN AFTER TONIGHT'S HANDIWORK!

AND IT'S THE SAME THING ALL THE WAY DOWN ROSSELL AVENUE.

A SEEDED RYE IN THE SMALLEST DAY-OLD BREAD STORE, TWENTY BLOCKS AWAY, WILL BE AFFECTED BY WHAT WE'RE DOING HERE THIS MORNING.

SANITARY BAKING CO.

DRY GOODS

I BETTER HURRY UP

GARDEN of EDEN

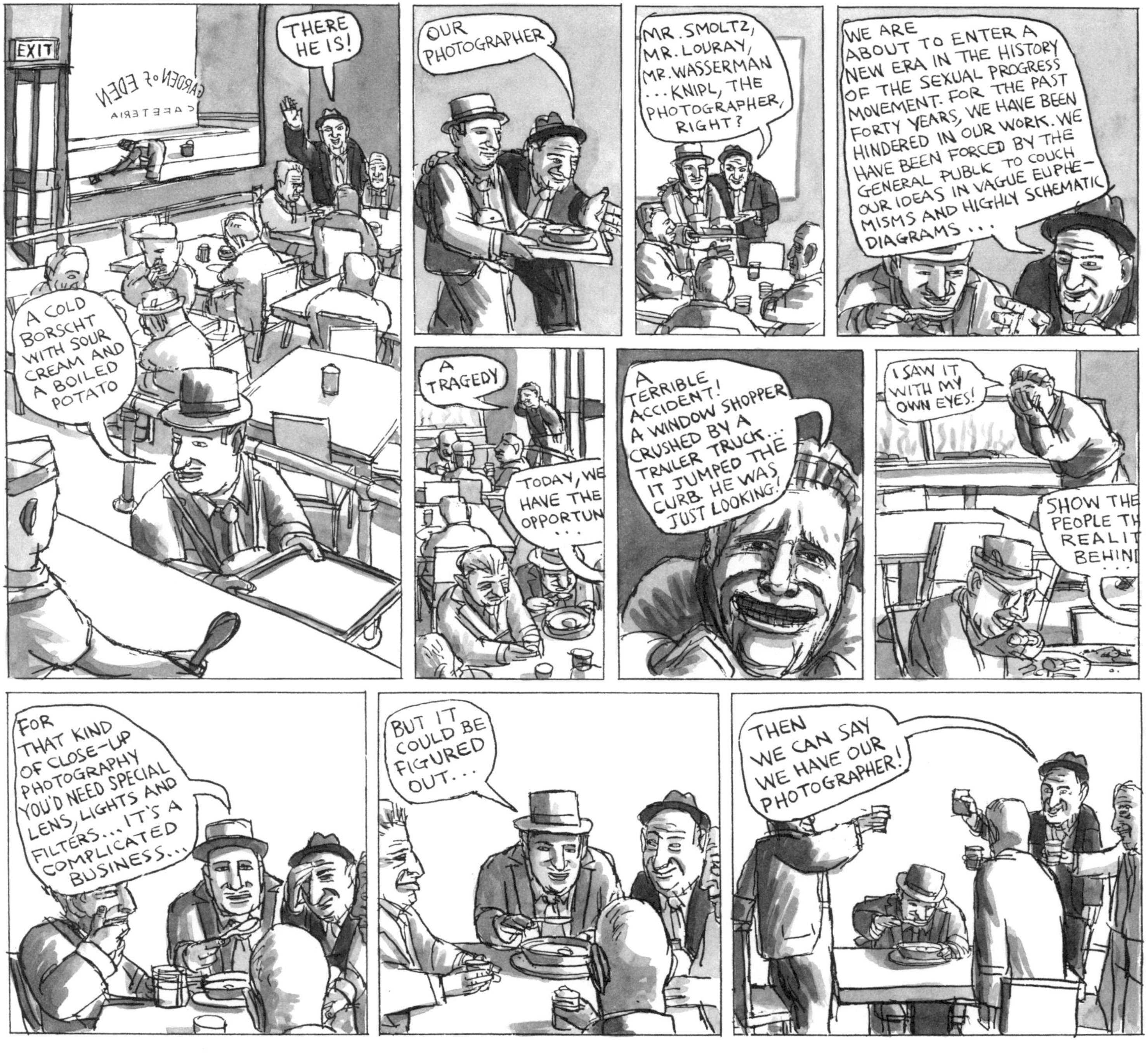
EXIT
GARDEN of EDEN CAFETERIA
THERE HE IS!
A COLD BORSCHT WITH SOUR CREAM AND A BOILED POTATO
OUR PHOTOGRAPHER.
MR. SMOLTZ, MR. LOURAY, MR. WASSERMAN ...KNIPL, THE PHOTOGRAPHER, RIGHT?
WE ARE ABOUT TO ENTER A NEW ERA IN THE HISTORY OF THE SEXUAL PROGRESS MOVEMENT. FOR THE PAST FORTY YEARS, WE HAVE BEEN HINDERED IN OUR WORK. WE HAVE BEEN FORCED BY THE GENERAL PUBLIC TO COUCH OUR IDEAS IN VAGUE EUPHEMISMS AND HIGHLY SCHEMATIC DIAGRAMS...
A TRAGEDY
-TODAY, WE HAVE THE OPPORTUN ...
A TERRIBLE ACCIDENT! A WINDOW SHOPPER CRUSHED BY A TRAILER TRUCK... IT JUMPED THE CURB. HE WAS JUST LOOKING!
I SAW IT WITH MY OWN EYES!
SHOW THE PEOPLE TH REALIT BEHIN ...
FOR THAT KIND OF CLOSE-UP PHOTOGRAPHY YOU'D NEED SPECIAL LENS, LIGHTS AND FILTERS... IT'S A COMPLICATED BUSINESS...
BUT IT COULD BE FIGURED OUT...
THEN WE CAN SAY WE HAVE OUR PHOTOGRAPHER!

FOR SUSIE TAUBE

DRAWNANDQUARTERLY.COM | KATCHOR.COM

First Drawn & Quarterly edition: September 2016 | Printed in China | 10 9 8 7 6 5 4 3 2 1

Cheap Novelties was originally published as a *RAW* one-shot by Penguin Books in 1991. The single page strips in this book originally appeared in the *New York Press* from April 20, 1988, to March 27, 1991.

Library and Archives Canada Cataloguing in Publication: Katchor, Ben author, artist. *Cheap Novelties: The Pleasures of Urban Decay*/ Ben Katchor. Originally published 1991. Features a new cover and comics from Katchor's tabloid newspaper *The Daily Pigeon*. ISBN 978-1-77046-263-2 (hardback) 1. Graphic novels—Comic books, strips, etc. I. Title. PN6727.K28C47 2016 741.5'973 C2016-900964-5

Published in the USA by Drawn & Quarterly, a client publisher of Farrar, Straus and Giroux. Orders: 888.330.8477. Published in Canada by Drawn & Quarterly, a client publisher of Raincoast Books. Orders: 800.663.5714. Published in the United Kingdom by Drawn & Quarterly, a client publisher of Publishers Group UK. Orders: info@pguk.co.uk.

Kasha
Knish

BEN KATCHOR is best know for his long-running comic-strip work—*Julius Knipl, Real Estate Photographer, The Cardboard Valise, Hotel & Farm, The Jew of New York,* and *Hand-Drying in America,* a collection of his monthly strips from *Metropolis* magazine. Katchor has also collaborated with musician Mark Mulcahy on a number of works for musical theatre, including *The Slug Bearers of Kayrol Island, The Rosenbach Company, A Checkroom Romance,* and *Up From the Stacks.* He has been the recipient of both a Guggenheim Fellowship and a MacArthur Fellowship. Katchor lives in New York, where he is an Associate Professor at Parsons School of Design—The New School. As director of Parsons' Illustration program, he runs The New York Comics & Picture-story Symposium, a weekly lecture series for the study of text-image work.

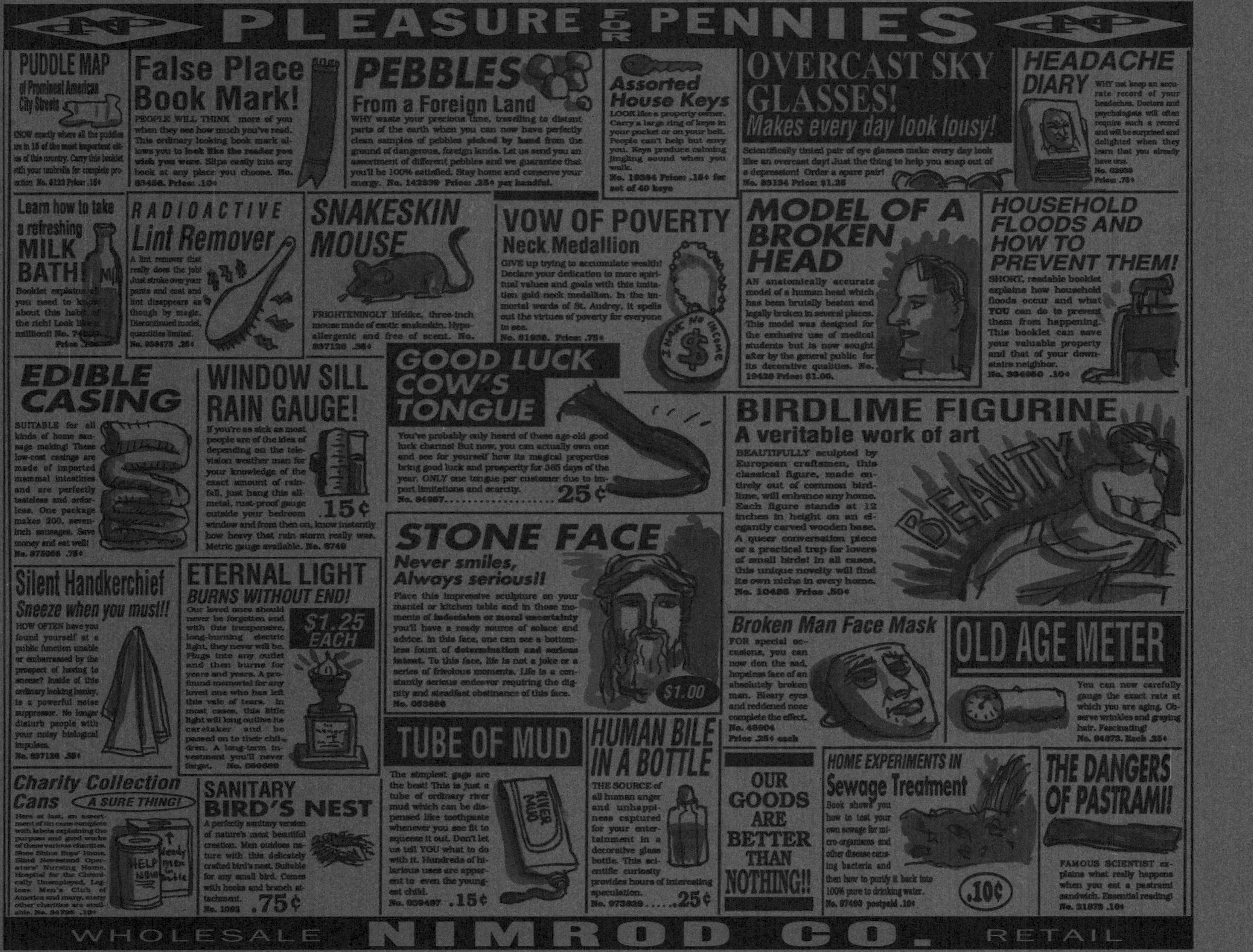
PLEASURE FOR PENNIES
PUDDLE MAP of Prominent American City Streets
KNOW exactly where all the puddles are in 15 of the most important cities of this country. Carry this booklet with your umbrella for complete protection. No. 8123 Price: .15¢
False Place Book Mark!
PEOPLE WILL THINK more of you when they see how much you've read. This ordinary looking book mark allows you to look like the reader you wish you were. Slips easily into any book at any place you choose. No. 83456. Price: .10¢
PEBBLES From a Foreign Land
WHY waste your precious time, travelling to distant parts of the earth when you can now have perfectly clean samples of pebbles picked by hand from the ground of dangerous, foreign lands. Let us send you an assortment of different pebbles and we guarantee that you'll be 100% satisfied. Stay home and conserve your energy. No. 142839 Price: .25¢ per handful.
Assorted House Keys
LOOK like a property owner. Carry a large ring of keys in your pocket or on your belt. People can't help but envy you. Keys produce calming jingling sound when you walk.
No. 19384 Price: .15¢ for set of 40 keys
OVERCAST SKY GLASSES!
Makes every day look lousy!
Scientifically tinted pair of eye glasses make every day look like an overcast day! Just the thing to help you snap out of a depression! Order a spare pair!
No. 83134 Price: $1.25
HEADACHE DIARY
WHY not keep an accurate record of your headaches. Doctors and psychologists will often require such a record and will be surprised and delighted when they learn that you already have one.
No. 02938
Price: .75¢
Learn how to take a refreshing MILK BATH!
Booklet explains
you need to
about this habit
the rich! Look
millionl! No.
Price
RADIOACTIVE Lint Remover
A lint remover that really does the job! Just stroke over your pants and coat and lint disappears as though by magic. Discontinued model, quantities limited.
No. 938473 .25¢
SNAKESKIN MOUSE
FRIGHTENINGLY lifelike, three-inch mouse made of exotic snakeskin. Hypo-allergenic and free of scent. No. 837126 .35¢
VOW OF POVERTY Neck Medallion
GIVE up trying to accumulate wealth! Declare your dedication to more spiritual values and goals with this imitation gold neck medallion. In the immortal words of St. Audrey, it spells out the virtues of poverty for everyone to see.
No. 81936. Price: .75¢
I HAVE NO INCOME
MODEL OF A BROKEN HEAD
AN anatomically accurate model of a human head which has been brutally beaten and legally broken in several places. This model was designed for the exclusive use of medical students but is now sought after by the general public for its decorative qualities. No. 19428 Price: $1.05.
HOUSEHOLD FLOODS AND HOW TO PREVENT THEM!
SHORT, readable booklet explains how household floods occur and what YOU can do to prevent them from happening. This booklet can save your valuable property and that of your downstairs neighbor.
No. 394050 .10¢
EDIBLE CASING
SUITABLE for all kinds of home sausage making! These low-cost casings are made of imported mammal intestines and are perfectly tasteless and ordorless. One package makes 200, seven-inch sausages. Save money and eat well!
No. 875966 .75¢
WINDOW SILL RAIN GAUGE!
If you're as sick as most people are of the idea of depending on the television weather man for your knowledge of the exact amount of rainfall, just hang this all-metal, rust-proof gauge outside your bedroom window and from then on, know instantly how heavy that rain storm really was. Metric gauge available. No. 6749
.15¢
GOOD LUCK COW'S TONGUE
You've probably only heard of these age-old good luck charms! But now, you can actually own one and see for yourself how its magical properties bring good luck and prosperity for 365 days of the year. ONLY one tongue per customer due to import limitations and scarcity.
No. 84957.................... 25¢
BIRDLIME FIGURINE
A veritable work of art
BEAUTIFULLY sculpted by European craftsmen, this classical figure, made entirely out of common birdlime, will enhance any home. Each figure stands at 12 inches in height on an elegantly carved wooden base. A queer conversation piece or a practical trap for lovers of small birds! In all cases, this unique novelty will find its own niche in every home.
No. 10488 Price .50¢
BEAUTY
STONE FACE
Never smiles, Always serious!!
Place this impressive sculpture on your mantel or kitchen table and in those moments of indecision or moral uncertainty you'll have a ready source of solace and advice. In this face, one can see a bottomless fount of determination and serious intent. To this face, life is not a joke or a series of frivolous moments. Life is a constantly serious endeavor requiring the dignity and steadfast obstinance of this face.
No. 053886
$1.00
Silent Handkerchief
Sneeze when you must!!
HOW OFTEN have you found yourself at a public function unable or embarrassed by the prospect of having to sneeze? Inside of this ordinary looking hanky, is a powerful noise suppressor. No longer disturb people with your noisy biological impulses.
No. 837126 .35¢
ETERNAL LIGHT
BURNS WITHOUT END!
Our loved ones should never be forgotten and with this inexpensive, long-burning electric light, they never will be. Plugs into any outlet and then burns for years and years. A profound memorial for any loved one who has left this vale of tears. In most cases, this little light will long outlive its caretaker and be passed on to their children. A long-term investment you'll never forget. No. 060680
$1.25 EACH
Broken Man Face Mask
FOR special occasions, you can now don the sad, hopeless face of an absolutely broken man. Bleary eyes and reddened nose complete the effect.
No. 48904
Price .25¢ each
OLD AGE METER
You can now carefully gauge the exact rate at which you are aging. Observe wrinkles and graying hair. Fascinating!
No. 94873. Each .25¢
Charity Collection Cans
A SURE THING!
Here at last, an assortment of tin cans complete with labels explaining the purpose and good works of these various charities. Shoe Shine Boys' Home, Blind Newsstand Operators' Nursing Home, Hospital for the Chronically Unemployed, Legless Men's Club of America and many, many other charities are available. No. 84728 .10¢
HELP NOW
Needy
SANITARY BIRD'S NEST
A perfectly sanitary version of nature's most beautiful creation. Man outdoes nature with this delicately crafted bird's nest. Suitable for any small bird. Comes with hooks and branch attachment.
No. 1062 .75¢
TUBE OF MUD
The simplest gags are the best! This is just a tube of ordinary river mud which can be dispensed like toothpaste whenever you see fit to squeeze it out. Don't let us tell YOU what to do with it. Hundreds of hilarious uses are apperent to even the youngest child.
No. 039487 .15¢
RIVER MUD
HUMAN BILE IN A BOTTLE
THE SOURCE of all human anger and unhappiness captured for your entertainment in a decorative glass bottle. This scientific curiosity provides hours of interesting speculation.
No. 973829.....25¢
OUR GOODS ARE BETTER THAN NOTHING!!
HOME EXPERIMENTS IN Sewage Treatment
Book shows you how to test your own sewage for micro-organisms and other disease causing bacteria and then how to purify it back into 100% pure to drinking water.
No. 87490 postpaid .10¢
.10¢
THE DANGERS OF PASTRAMI!
FAMOUS SCIENTIST explains what really happens when you eat a pastrami sandwich. Essential reading!
No. 21873 .10¢
WHOLESALE NIMROD CO. RETAIL